Lele's Selah

Prayerful Poems that Inspire Hope

Lele Beutel

Copyright © 2020 by Winnowing Words

All rights reserved.

Scripture quotations are taken from the Holy Bible, New Living Translation, copyright © 1996, 2004. Used by permission of Tyndale House Publishers, Inc., Carol Stream, Illinois 60188. All rights reserved.

No portion of this book may be reproduced in any form without written permission from the publisher or author, except as permitted by U.S. copyright law.

Lele Beutel loves to meet and chat with fans! Reach out to her at apedersen6@comcast.net.

Book Cover by Tatiana Vila

Paperback ISBN: 979-8-646-18554-0
Hardcover ISBN: 979-8-9902359-4-6
Ebook ISBN: 978-0-578-69679-9

To those who long to feel the heartbeat of God

Foreword

Like a heartbeat, a poem can support and sustain life. The cadence of a poem is like the beat of a heart, set in motion by God Himself. Often He wakes me up in the middle of the night with words, even a whole verse, to put to pen. If I'm willing, and motivated enough, I will rise up and write the words on a page—the beginnings of a new poem to honor Him. In the past, I'd get up early in the morning to walk around a lake for an hour to experience the quiet solitude of time just with Him. It was during these precious moments that I prayed for others and myself, and asked Him many questions. He often answered me, not with straight-forward replies, but with pictures. And the scenes He relayed worked themselves into poems, which I wrote down later. This book is made up of many of the "heartbeats" He gave me during these times. Some come in the form of rhymes, some are word-thoughts, some are prayers, and some are praises. Some are from my point of view. Others are from His.

What is the meaning of the word, *"selah?"* *GotQuestions.org* concludes: "The Amplified Bible adds 'pause and calmly think about that' to each verse where *selah* appears. When we see the word *selah* in a psalm or in Habakkuk 3, we should pause to carefully weigh the meaning of what we have just read or heard, lifting up our hearts in praise to God for His great truths. 'All the earth bows down to you; they sing praise to you, they sing the praises of your name. *Selah!*' (Psalm 66:4)."[1]

The essence of *selah* can be relayed through the depths of a psalm, a song, a praise, or a poem. In *Streams in the Desert*, the book's author discloses the following sentiment: "Is there any word in the Psalms more eloquent than the word 'Selah,' meaning pause? Is there anything more thrilling and awe-inspiring than the calm before the crashing of the storm, or the strange quiet that seems to

---

1. "What does selah mean in the Bible," GotQuestions.org.

fall upon nature before some supernatural phenomenon or disastrous upheaval? And is there anything that can touch our hearts like the *power of stillness*? For the hearts that will cease focusing on themselves, there is 'the peace of God, which transcends all understanding' (Phil.4:7); 'quietness and trust' (Isa. 30:15), which is the source of all strength; a 'great peace' that will never 'make them stumble' (Ps. 119:165); and a deep rest, which the world can never give nor take away. Deep within the center of the soul is a chamber of peace where God lives and where, if we will enter it and quiet all the other sounds, we can hear His 'gentle whisper' (I Kings 19:12). Even in the fastest wheel that is turning, if you look at the center, where the axle is found, there is no movement at all. And even in the busiest life, there is a place where we may dwell alone with God in eternal stillness. There is only one way to know God: 'Be still, and know.' 'The Lord is in his holy temple; let all the earth be silent before him' (Hab. 2:20)."[2]

I have separated the poems of this book into three sections, because three represents completeness. The first section demonstrates the dawning of His light in your life. It shows the place and time when He first comes to you, wherever you may be. Here, He makes Himself known to you. It may be a day in spring, a summer day, a fall day, or a dreary winter day. But He will always make Himself known to you through the world you live in when you are ready to receive Him.

The second section is the life He desires for you on earth, now that you know Who He is. It's the life He seeks for you, but also how you live your life with Him. It's the struggle up the mountain, which sometimes seems hard and grueling and painful, but issues in His great and abundant peace and serenity, and a breathtaking view once the peak is attained. It's your journey.

The third section describes where we will all be when He returns for us. It's the final destination, the awe-inspiring mountaintop, so to speak. It's our new life, one day, with Him beside us. It's our ultimate hope.

Please allow the scripture references to add value as you "dig deeper" into the meaning of each shared verse. And as you read each poem, let Him speak to you, as He spoke to me...through a heartbeat. Let them simmer, let them work their "magic" on your own heart. Let them heal your hurts and wounds, and take you to a new place—a place of worship and adoration for Him. How He loves you! How He adores you and wants to work through you. How He wants you to know His desire—to will and to do of His good pleasure in you (Philippians 2:13).

Allow a pause, a stillness, a *selah*, in your busy day. Let the words of these praise-filled poems sink into your heart and prepare it for your future life—the one you long for. My hope for you is to achieve a fulfilling destination of peace and love and joy now, and a new life with Him one day. May your journey be sweet, with Him working in and through you!
—Lele Beutel, 2024

---

2. November 24, *Streams in the Desert*, 366 Daily Devotional Readings, L.B. Cowman, edited by James Reimann, ePub Format, Copyright © 1996 by Zondervan.

How He adores you!

Come alive, because of what He did for you.

"For this is how God loved the world: He gave his one and only Son, so that everyone who believes in him will not perish but have eternal life."

—JOHN 3:16

Light

"Light shines on the godly, and joy on those whose hearts are right."
—Psalm 97:11

Light binds
like an egg.
It holds
and coheres
through love.

Darkness divides
like a wall.
It separates
and forces out
light.

Magic

*"Ask me and I will tell you remarkable secrets
you do not know about things to come."
—Jeremiah 33:3*

There is a sense of magic
in every plant we see,
in every bird and creature,
in every blooming tree.
One can't but ask in wonder,
"How did they come to be?
And, who is their creator,
whose hand now holds the key?"
We search through every answer
to understand fully,
and if we stop to question,
it isn't hard to see.
The One Who cared to make these,
the Same Who planted me,
has been around for ages,
and sets our destiny.
He speaks through words eternal.
He offers spiritual seeds.
And in His hand is "magic"
for those who will believe.

How Can I Believe?

"Go out and stand before me on the mountain," the LORD told him. And as Elijah stood there, the LORD passed by, and a mighty windstorm hit the mountain. It was such a terrible blast that the rocks were torn loose, but the LORD was not in the wind. After the wind there was an earthquake, but the LORD was not in the earthquake. And after the earthquake there was a fire, but the LORD was not in the fire. And after the fire there was the sound of a gentle whisper."
—I Kings 19:11-12

How can I believe,
when all around me fails,
and people I love so
have devastating ails?
Are You the rock or what?
Can You deliver peace?
We see so many hate,
and killings never cease.
It's hard to see Your love.
We patiently await,
as our own earth dissolves
into a ruined state.
But then I hear Your voice,
not in the storm or wind,
but in my heart it sounds,
with whispered words again.
You tell me how Your love
cannot be found in greed,
or lust, or selfish gain,
but in a small child's need.

When others look away
from their own wants and hate,
and criticism strong,
to seek another gate,
through it alone they find
a place that's filled with peace,
a garden made for good,
where strivings finally cease,
where beauty can exist,
and pleasantness abounds,
where You are in the midst,
and Your kind words are found.

Ruts

"God places the lonely in families; he sets the prisoners free and gives them joy. But he makes the rebellious live in a sun-scorched land."
—Psalm 68:6

In a rut,
we may not budge,
repeating words
from hate-filled grudges.
Constantly bucking
God's design,
always lacking joy,
we whine.
And little do we
understand
that from the start,
God has a plan.
We could fulfill
a heavenly call,
if we'd but turn
from our own gall.
He beckons to us,
calls our name.
We turn away
with great disdain.
But He continues
in His quest
to reach our hearts
and give us rest.
And sadly it

so happens often—
it's not until
we reach rock-bottom
that we in our
exasperation
turn to Him
for restoration.
From our grief
and sadness borne,
we finally ask
for help, forlorn.
And He in His own
patience, kindness,
forgives us of
our blatant blindness,
accepts us, heals us,
pulls us in.
For prodigal ones
new life begins.
And if we'll stay,
and not give up,
we'll see His goodness
as we sup.
His table laden
with plenty in store,
is more than enough
to fill our core.
His hand bestowing
tenderness sure
overflows with love
and so much more.

What's Hidden

"He reveals deep and mysterious things and knows what lies hidden in darkness, though he is surrounded by light."
—Daniel 2:22

What's hidden beneath the surface
may belie what covers all.
I may seem so "together,"
but getting ready for a fall.
Fancy clothes and jewelry
cover hurtful pride.
Well-styled hair and make-up
mask what lies inside.
Lord, would You reveal
if You behold a lack,
if my heart's lifted up,
or the devil's on my back.
I may be too proud to see it,
trying hard to issue blame,
when the actual, true problem
rides on me, causing shame.

True Eyes

"The godly people in the land are my true heroes! I take pleasure in them!"
—Psalm 16:3

To put a human face on it
requires humility.
It means that one must listen,
and requires the ability
to see below the surface,
and notice what's around,
to look beyond mere words,
and gaze beneath the ground.
And with true eyes of gratitude,
it requires a certain discernment—
perception beyond the common,
love unfathomable and yearning.
Only a few significant ones
attain this ability—
to be able to dig down deep
beneath the layers peeled.
How thankful we all should be
for those who are not shaken,
who turn the tide of history
by courage unmistaken.

What is Prosperity to You?

"The LORD gives his people strength. The LORD blesses them with peace."
—Psalm 29:11

Prosperity means
different things
to different people.
To some,
prosperity means
having a large house
with fancy furniture
and gold lamps with fancy tassels,
and lush carpeting—
the kind that feels squishy under your toes.
It means having
a shiny car with leather seats,
and a sun roof,
and a blaring stereo system.
It means dining
in fine restaurants,
where waiters dress up
in bow ties with crisp white shirts,
and polished black shoes.
To others,
prosperity means
having money to travel—
being able to sit on the deck

of a large cruise ship,
sailing through crystal waters,
watching whales and dolphins,
and islands with palm trees,
seeing white-plastered homes
with red-tiled roofs,
where children peer through windows
at white sandy beaches.
To others,
prosperity means
visiting family members,
driving through cities and towns,
along highways,
through mountains and valleys,
forests and fields,
to faraway places,
where small faces
greet them at doors,
and give them hugs,
and are excited to see them
at last.
To others,
prosperity means
friendship—
having people who accept
and love them,
and bring them casseroles
when they are sick,
or send cards
when they are sad,
who will call to see
how they are doing,
and are willing to talk
for hours
on the phone,
or come over
to play games,
and laugh and share stories
together,
who will drink with them—
beer or wine, coffee or tea,
and sit with them
whenever they need it.
To others,
prosperity means
having peace.

It means having a relationship
sought through pain
and patience.
It means embracing a place
of the heart.
It means a feeling
of being home at last,
no matter where they are.
It is rest.
This kind of prosperity
can only be found
in Him.

When I Was Wee

*"And we are confident that he hears us whenever
we ask for anything that pleases him."*
—I John 5:14

When I was wee,
I desired approval.
Acknowledgement was
the aim of my being.
I wanted so much
to be loved and encouraged,
and, finally, not subtly, be seen.
As time went by,
and people ignored me,
focusing on their own pressing needs,
I realized that only
One really heard me—
my requests, my desires, my pleas.
It may be to you very frustrating,
day by day, night by night,
as you speak to deaf ears.
At some point you'll see,
just as I did,
only One is tuned into your fears.
Bring your needs,
your desires and dreams,
to this One Who longs to hear

your unnoticed voice
lifted up to Him.
With approval, He'll shed a tear
as He listens to you.

Are You Different?

"You are not like that, for you are a chosen people. You are royal priests, a holy nation, God's very own possession. As a result, you can show others the goodness of God, for he called you out of the darkness into his wonderful light."
—I Peter 2:9

Do you feel that you are different,
and you just do not fit in?
Do you sometimes feel rejected
for a lack of social kin?
Does your heart feel raw and ready,
pounding loudly, but no one hears?
Do your eyes perpetually gaze out,
seeking love instead of tears?
Did you know that Someone seeks you,
to reveal His heart's bequest.
He has sought you from conception,
picked you out from all the rest.
It is true that you are different,
and you never will fit in.
You were chosen for another,
other-worldly family bin.
Turn and look upon Him—
He's your Lover; He's your Friend.
It is He Who just adores you,
heals your heart, restores again.
Then in peace you'll finally see
that you always did belong,
and forever will fit in
to an unseen body strong.

Meant for Love

*"From there you will search again for the LORD your God.
And if you search for him with all your heart and soul, you will find him."*
—Deuteronomy 4:29

Why stay in pity's puddle,
where all your thoughts are self,
and life is one big muddle
of lies and fear and stealth?

Why not face life's challenge
with what is true instead—
that you are meant for love,
a new love you can wed?

This love extends beyond you,
and all your inward fears.
Its greatness can uplift you,
and dry your flood of tears.

Can you not see its wonder
in the natural world around,
through life and all its seasons,
and the goodness that surrounds?

If you will but awaken
from your necrotic sleep,
and open up your eyes,
and clear them from your weeping...

You'll see what's made from light—
this love you have not known
and all the gifts it brings—
life-giving new seeds sown.

This love speaks to you now:
"Come and walk with Me."
It reaches for your hand,
but you must turn to see.

Wouldn't It?

"Let your roots grow down into him, and let your lives be built on him. Then your faith will grow strong in the truth you were taught, and you will overflow with thankfulness."
—*Colossians 2:7*

Wouldn't it be prudent,
wouldn't it be wise,
to lift our hearts in gladness
than otherwise surmise?

Wouldn't it bequeath us,
wouldn't it be true,
that a heart brimful of sadness
is sorrowfully imbued?

Couldn't we deal truly,
couldn't we decide,
in thankfulness to live,
in joyfulness to ride?

Wouldn't we be happy,
wouldn't we be blessed,
to lean on His pure beauty,
and on His arm to rest?

Wouldn't it be heavenly,
wouldn't it be great,
to see the way that He sees,
to love instead of hate?

A Battle

*"The horse is prepared for the day of battle,
but the victory belongs to the LORD."*
—Proverbs 21:31

Your own children
have struggled
and sighed
and fought
and died,
trying to attain
a place of beauty,
a rest, a peace,
where their struggles
would dissolve and cease.
We are in a battle.
Because of Adam,
we fight for our souls,
while longing for heaven.
Digging out of holes,
we seek pleasures
that come and go.
Here for a moment,
they expire at death.
Though pursuits are fervent,
only through You
can we have real peace—
the beauty we seek
by humbling ourselves,
with hearts that are meek.

Be near us today,
as struggles prevail.
Walk by our side
through showers of hail,
that in You we may abide.

Why?

"I am ignored as if I were dead, as if I were a broken pot."
—*Psalm 31:12*

Sadness, sullenness,
draining soul of life,
since others have forgotten
your love
poured out to them
through actions, tears, empathy.
And you need them now
to show some kindness,
to remember
a card, a call,
a word, an appearance,
an embrace.
But they are nowhere,
caught up
in their own worlds,
in their own busyness,
oblivious
to you.
And you cry,
and sulk,
and entertain
self-pity
for awhile,
until
you are sick of it.
Then you finally

turn to Him
and ask,
Why?
Why are so many
so far away?
And He answers you,
Because
I want your love
for Me.
I want your focus
on Me now.

I want you
to know
how much I love you,
and always have.
Before you were born
I picked you out,
because I adored you,
and counted you as special,
unique.
You are precious
to Me—
a gem,
the apple of My eye.
I separated you out
from others
and made you
different.
So now
you see—
I made others blind
to your beauty,
because I wanted
you to see
how beautiful
you are to Me.

He Seeks

*"The LORD looks down from heaven on the entire human race;
he looks to see if anyone is truly wise, if anyone seeks God."*
—*Psalm 14:2*

I seek a godly man,
whose heart with Me does flow,
whose words are filled with truth
and kindness, blessings sown.

I seek a godly woman,
whose tenderness and zeal
support and usher in
the fragrance of appeal.

I seek a godly child,
whose meekness unsurpassed,
with humbleness, prevails
through every God-sent task.

I seek a godly land,
whose heart is lifted up
to Me in prayer-spent hours,
while dining with Me sups.

Favor

"For whoever finds me finds life and receives favor from the Lord."
—Proverbs 8:35

The favor of the Lord
rests solidly on those
whose heart in Him does trust,
whose frightfulness is deposed,
whose mind escapes the dust,
whose thoughts on Him do rest,
whose actions celebrate
the reality of what is best.

Speak to Me

"Guide my steps by your word, so I will not be overcome by evil."
—Psalm 119:133

Speak to me in moments,
when anxiety seems to reign,
and time-tested, God-sent precepts
are exchanged for a moment's gain.

Remind me of Your wisdom
and understanding ways,
when people seem to flee to
confusion in a haze.

Enlighten me in Your path,
when no one seems to know,
and blindly others walk
someplace where they must go.

Guide me toward deliverance,
when all the world is trapped,
and many keep on yelling
for more, their own hands strapped.

Touch me with Your mercy,
when merciless ones lead,
and talk about their kindness,
while others cry and bleed.

Expectations

*"The hopes of the godly result in happiness,
but the expectations of the wicked come to nothing."
—Proverbs 10:28*

Expectations are resentments
in a premeditated state,
when we're expecting others
to similarly relate.
We're often disappointed
when it's nothing we receive,
and we've given ourselves completely,
and we've spent our time believing
that someday they'll return
our thoughtful kindness shared,
and our own day will come—
we'll see how much they cared.
But it's certain we'll be sad,
if we expect a sure response.
Most are too consumed
with their own compelling bonds.
So, we give to Him instead,
and respond to His bestowing.
Then it's sure that we'll have hope
and a certainty in knowing
that we are truly loved,
and appreciated still.
And our expectations dashed
are by His love fulfilled!

Desperation

*"In my desperation I prayed, and the LORD listened;
he saved me from all my troubles."*
—*Psalm 34:6*

Groping for You
in desperation,
when all I want
is to crawl away.
When the world is unkind,
and the media blares,
and I just want
to feel Your embrace.
When others push me
farther and farther away,
to greater distances,
from them,
I'll bow before
Your uplifting spirit.
I'll sing Your songs,
and hum Your hymns.
You're the reason
I exist.
You're the Shelter
in the storm.
You're my high Tower,
My Lighthouse.
You're the reason
I was born.
You alone

can help and quiet,
when all around me
shout and hurl.
Your words encourage.
Be near me now
as I once again
walk into the world.

A Little

"Go and celebrate with a feast of rich foods and sweet drinks, and share gifts of food with people who have nothing prepared. This is a sacred day before the Lord. Don't be dejected and sad, for the joy of the LORD is your strength!"
—*Nehemiah 8:10*

A little rest,
a great deal of joy,
a bit of zest,
to uplift the soul.
A little peace
can help and heal,
and bring release,
when burdens mount.

Mercy

"O Lord, you are so good, so ready to forgive,
so full of unfailing love for all who ask for your help."
—Psalm 86:5

Seeking Your mercy,
when mercy has failed.
Seeking Your joy,
when sorrows prevail.
Seeking Your goodness,
when the world assails.
Seeking Your wisdom,
when foolishness hails.
Seeking Your kindness,
when harsh words travail.

Grace

"My grace is all you need. My power works best in weakness."
—*II Corinthians 12:9*

Give me joy
when I feel depressed.
Give me peace
when I'm overwhelmed.
Give me humility
when I begin to feel too proud.
Give me goodness
when my thoughts stray away.
Give me grace to love
when I don't feel like loving.
Give me mercy
when I am unkind.
Give me forgiveness
when I fall short.

Peace

*"In peace I will lie down and sleep, for you alone,
O LORD, will keep me safe."*
—Psalm 4:8

I seek Your peace, Lord, in all I feel.
I seek Your love, Lord, in all I say.
I seek your gentleness, Lord, in all I do.

You, Lord, are all righteousness, power, and holiness.
You give us life and bless us mightily.
You are ever-present.

Thank you for being here now for me.
Thank you for blessing my day and helping me to maintain peace.
Thank you for the ability to be loving, kind, and to walk with You.

Only You can give me the strength to do this.
Only You can give me the peace I seek.
Only You can love me, even when I fall short.

Crystal Clear

"Give thanks to him who made the heavenly lights. His faithful love endures forever. The sun to rule the day. His faithful love endures forever. And the moon and stars to rule the night. His faithful love endures forever."
—Psalm 136:7-9

Crystal clear,
the stars shine bright,
beckoning to me
in the black of night.
Sometimes shooting
from here to there—
fountains of water
unparalleled.
Sparkling and winking,
blinking their light,
radiating gladness
in reds, blues, and whites.
Brilliantly gleaming,
like gems in the sky—
diamonds and rubies,
and pearls of great price.
Forming patterns
of warriors and queens,
swords and dragons,
godly scenes.
And I am reminded
of Your story told
in the stars, in the night,
for all to behold.

Gold

"Timely advice is lovely like golden apples in a silver basket."
—*Proverbs 25:11*

Like apples of gold
in baskets of silver,
Your wisdom brightens,
enlightens, delivers.
Should we be slaves
to things that we choose?
Can we be freed
by the good things we do?
Only through You
can our choices be
ones that enliven,
help, and set free.

Unveil

"I will delight in your decrees and not forget your word."
—*Psalm 119:16*

Direct me to Your Word,
for it is my delight.
Let it stir my mind,
removing every fright.
Reveal to me its depth.
Uncover mysteries.
Unravel every layer,
until its core I seize.
Clothe me in its grace.
Drape me endlessly.
As I walk forth today,
unveil my eyes to see.

A Beautiful Design

"We know that God causes everything to work together for the good of those who love God and are called according to his purpose for them."
—*Romans 8:28*

Memories of life
like stories intertwine,
woven by our God
with workmanship divine.
He takes what seems uncertain
and sews and weaves it so
that a beautiful design
emerges and unfolds.
When we show ourselves lacking,
or stumble, or careen,
He lays hold of our shortcomings
and creates a brand new scene.
We wonder and we ponder
how bad can become good.
It's only through His skill
that it ever could.
Don't worry if your weakness
seems to overwhelm,
or others do berate you
through unkindness or through stealth.
Just remember Joseph,
when cruelty was afoot.
God worked the details out
for everybody's good.

Reach

"His purpose was for the nations to seek after God and perhaps feel their way toward him and find him—though he is not far from any one of us."
—*Acts 17:27*

Reach up to Me for healing.
Reach up to Me for answers.
Reach up to Me for fellowship.
Reach up to Me for forgiveness.
My kind hands are held out to you.

Bounteous

"Look at the birds. They don't plant or harvest or store food in barns, for your heavenly Father feeds them. And aren't you far more valuable to him than they are?"
—Matthew 6:26

I will give in kindness
what you may fail to see,
as you busily encounter
a life of scarcity.
With your eyes on pure survival,
fixed ahead on what you need,
you cannot recognize
the blessings straight from Me.
Continually I pour down
everything you need,
but you worry and you stew still,
wondering what you'll drink or eat.
For the sparrow I provide
bounteous grass and seed,
there are always good provisions
if you'll simply trust in Me.

Surrender

"Seek the Kingdom of God above all else, and live righteously, and he will give you everything you need."
—Matthew 6:33

Surrender yourself.
Surrender your fears,
your cares, your worries.
Dine at My table.
Eat of My abundance.
Allow your mind to be at peace,
by putting on My thoughts,
My ways.
Let Me surround you with My joy,
and comfort you with My kindness.
Surrender your concerns.
Let Me envelop you in My love,
for My love is great—
more than you can comprehend.
Know that it surpasses
all human love.
Think of how you love your children,
your grandchildren.
Then magnify that a hundredfold,
a thousandfold.
That is My love for you.
So surrender yourself
to My love today.

My Promises to You

"Be still, and know that I am God!"
—Psalm 46:10

Wait for Me...
I will fulfill My promises to you.
Look to Me...
I will show Myself strong for you.
Reach for Me...
I will help you in times of trouble.
Gaze on Me...
I will reveal My true beauty to you.
Walk with Me...
I will guide your steps to good things.
Surrender to Me...
I will resurrect your life through Mine.
Depend on Me...
I will exhibit My power over the enemy.
Stand by Me...
I will protect you with My covering wings.
Rest in Me...
I will encompass you with peace and comfort.

Relax in Me

"For all who have entered into God's rest have rested from their labors, just as God did after creating the world."
—Hebrews 4:10

Relax in Me.
Rest in My presence.
Allow Me to flow through you,
bringing you peace, healing, and revival.
Trust Me with all your thoughts and feelings.
I can soothe your nerves and comfort you,
beyond any solace you have ever,
ever experienced in this world.
I am a God of restoration,
consolation, and love.
Let Me heal you
now.

Through

"When you go through deep waters, I will be with you. When you go through rivers of difficulty, you will not drown. When you walk through the fire of oppression, you will not be burned up; the flames will not consume you."
—Isaiah 43:2

Through tiring trials,
I show Myself strongest.
Through frightful fears,
I will prevail.

Through sickening sorrows,
My help runs deepest.
Through shocking storms,
I never fail.

Through long lost love,
My love is plenteous.
Through striking sickness,
My touch survives.

Through crushing cruelty,
My care increases.
Through threat of death,
life with Me thrives.

My Redemptive Rs

"The Holy Spirit produces this kind of fruit in our lives: love, joy, peace, patience, kindness, goodness, faithfulness, gentleness, and self-control. There is no law against these things!"
—*Galatians 5:22-23*

Be reborn with My Spirit.
Be renewed by My Word.
Be requited with My love.
Be rejuvenated by My joy.
Be rested through My peace.
Be responsive to My kindness.
Be revitalized with My goodness.
Be reconciled through My patience.
Be restored through My faithfulness.
Be refreshed through My gentleness.

A Song

"Sing a new song to the LORD! Let the whole earth sing to the LORD!"
—*Psalm 96:1*

It is a song of sorrow.
It is a song of joy—
a song to sing tomorrow
and today employ.

It speaks of death and grieving.
It speaks of life and love—
a song of godly seeking
and fragrance from above.

It heralds a new message.
It brings us an old story—
a song of heartfelt courage
and amazing glory.

It's never ceased to capture.
It's never missed a mark—
a song of hope and rapture
with a celestial spark.

A New Way

*"The thief's purpose is to steal and kill and destroy.
My purpose is to give them a rich and satisfying life."*
—John 10:10

The way of the world
is broad and common.
The path seems easy,
as its own god summons.
But another Way,
though steep at times,
is a Way of life,
magnificent, sublime.
And the Lord of this Way,
never ordering its members,
is a Lord of life,
loving and tender.

There Was a Wealthy Man...

"Since we are receiving a kingdom that is unshakable, let us be thankful and please God by worshiping him with holy fear and awe."
—Hebrews 12:28

There was a wealthy man,
who lived in a large home.
He prospered and abounded.
He never was alone.
But right next door to him,
a poor man suffered so.
He could not get around.
He had no place to go.
The wealthy man felt bad.
He had so very much.
His heart went out to him,
whose poverty was such.
He watched him withering,
stuck in his little cave.
He decided he must act,
and so to him he gave
one of his many cars
to get around, you see,
so the poor man could go
and travel, just like he.

He gave him cash for gas,
and food, and clothing too.
He gave him a charge card
to buy what he might choose.
He then was so elated,
glad for what he'd done.
He treated the poor man
like he was his own son.
But then the needy neighbor
took all these very things—
the gifts he had been given—
and chose to turn them in.
He traded in the car
for wine and drugs and beer.
And then he went and bought
a ticket to a seer.

He cashed the charge card in,
maxed out to the extreme.
He used the money then
for methamphetamines.
The rich man watched this scene
in anger and in pain.
He'd hoped the man would change,
being blessed by all he gave.
Instead the gifts were squandered
in harmful, thoughtless ways.
The poor man became poorer.
The rich man was dismayed.
It is a lesson well
of what God's for us done.
He gave us a precious gift—
His own beloved son.
And often, when we're needy,
He reaches out His hand,
then we squander what He gives
to live the life we've planned.
He tries to bless us so,
and gives us many things.
We do not see the price
of His great offerings.
We ignore the costly gifts
He sometimes pours on us.
And we remain so poor,
when He's magnanimous.

Oh, Lord, please let me see
what You have done for me.
Let me not be so blind
to this reality!

Precious

"He gave up his divine privileges; he took the humble position of a slave and was born as a human being. When he appeared in human form, he humbled himself in obedience to God and died a criminal's death on a cross. Therefore, God elevated him to the place of highest honor and gave him the name above all other names."
—Philippians 2:7-9

Precious peace,
bought with hardship,
when others turned
to forfeit grace.

Special love,
given lavishly,
when many lacked
the will to give.

Merciful pardon,
offered freely,
when many refused
to pay the price.

Unfathomable

"All praise to God, the Father of our Lord Jesus Christ, who has blessed us with every spiritual blessing in the heavenly realms because we are united with Christ."
—*Ephesians 1:3*

Unfathomable forgiveness...
I would receive it now.
Amazing assurance...
of Your once-spoken vow.
Magnanimous mercy...
holding back what I deserved.
Gratuitous grace...
Your favor undeserved.
Sacred sacrifice...
a gift of life so given.
Consecrated calling...
looking to You, may I be driven.

A Dream

"Store your treasures in heaven, where moths and rust cannot destroy, and thieves do not break in and steal."
—Matthew 6:20

Last night I dreamed a dream
of a family so proud.
They lived in a large house,
surrounded by a shroud.
They dressed in costly clothes.
They ate around a table.
They saw their servants come.
They thought that they were able.
They praised each others' worth—
the powers of their name,
the money they'd acquired
by playing the world's games.
I realized then that I
was party to this crowd.
I'd married the eldest son.
I'd spoken a solemn vow.
Now I lived by their own rules.
I must acknowledge and obey.
But I saw a problem here,
living with them each day.
Above the doorways there,
looking closely I could see
small, hidden monitors
they'd planted secretly.
They espied all goings out

and all the comings in,
and where each person went,
and where they did begin.
It was all a scheme of fear,
a world of sowed distrust.
To control what they could see
was to them a valid must.
I looked closer at their house,
haven of "security."
I found fissures in the walls
and cracks beneath my feet.
The wallpaper began to shred,
and the paint was chipped and peeled.
Under the carpeting,
wooden holes were now revealed.
It became more clear to me
what God showed me in this dream.
Money doesn't give us peace,
nor does fame or self-esteem.
Though the family was kind
and polite and mannerly,
their fear was soon unveiled
for loss of all their things.
What can give us peace of mind
lies not in what we see
or touch or hear or taste
or collect with brevity.
There's only One Who can,
when all is said and done.
He was indeed a Man.
He was Jesus, God's own Son.

Stardust

"The sun has one kind of glory, while the moon and stars each have another kind. And even the stars differ from each other in their glory."
—*I Corinthians 15:41*

You are made of stardust,
and your eyes are made for light,
as you gaze upon a rainbow,
and exclaim in pure delight,
as you reach for your high calling
and your utmost destiny,
as you wish upon a star,
thinking this will meet your need.
It's not "out there" as you think.
It's not in "the far beyond."
It can live right here within you,
where the Morning Star will dawn.
Stripping back the cloudy earthdust,
you can view the true beauty
of a living, breathing being,
and with star-struck eyes you'll see,
not the mud that you are made of,
quickly sinking with each day,
but the stardust in your fabric.
That's what lives and never fades!

To You

"It is the LORD who provides the sun to light the day and the moon and stars to light the night, and who stirs the sea into roaring waves. His name is the LORD of Heaven's Armies...."
—*Jeremiah 31:35*

Think of the stars,
how they brighten the night,
shining with pleasure,
emitting their light.
They twinkle, they sparkle.
They wink with delight,
because they emblazon
with powerful might.
Through ages they glimmer.
Through lightyears they live.
They rarely diminish.
True colors they give.
Your life is resplendent
with the light that He brings.
And you can illumine,
as you spread your wings.

Reach for a Rainbow

*"For I fully expect and hope that I will never be ashamed....
And I trust that my life will bring honor...whether I live or die."
—Philippians 1:20*

I do not want to dread today
or miss the joy of now.
I'd rather live without dismay
or doomsday thoughts somehow.

I do not want to fear the morrow,
or the dark unknown.
I'd rather live without this sorrow,
or its sadness sown.

Replace this darkness with Your light.
Replace this fear with faith.
Stir up new confidences bright.
Meet me at hope's hewn gate!

Hope's Gate

*"For I fully expect and hope that I will never be ashamed....
And I trust that my life will bring honor...whether I live or die."
—Philippians 1:20*

I do not want to dread today
or miss the joy of now.
I'd rather live without dismay
or doomsday thoughts somehow.

I do not want to fear the morrow,
or the dark unknown.
I'd rather live without this sorrow,
or its sadness sown.

Replace this darkness with Your light.
Replace this fear with faith.
Stir up new confidences bright.
Meet me at hope's hewn gate!

Integrity

"God is my shield, saving those whose hearts are true and right."
—Psalm 7:10

Give me salve
that I may see,
clothing white
that covers me.

In You I'm rich
with wealth that's real.
This I beseech—
Your majesty.

How can I win,
a victor be,
live in Your love,
integrity?

My soul is flesh,
my thoughts of earth.
Renew my vows
in second birth.

You are my Guard,
my rearward Shield.
I seek new faith—
integrity.

A Pearl

"This means that anyone who belongs to Christ has become a new person. The old life is gone; a new life has begun!"
—II Corinthians 5:17

I seek a rest
far from this world.
I seek a place
not found on earth.
The peace I seek
looks like a pearl,
held in a shell
of highest worth.
It draws me in,
within its circle—
a womb of light,
a second birth.
And I escape
and am interred
just long enough
to feel rebirth.
When I emerge,
I can rehearse
His ways of love—
life-changing words.

Keep Asking

"Keep on asking, and you will receive what you ask for. Keep on seeking, and you will find. Keep on knocking, and the door will be opened to you."
—Matthew 7:7

Some lack the persistence
that's needed with prayer
to see the results,
to feel healing there.
They pray only once
or twice or times three,
expecting immediate
response to their needs.
They don't understand
that by asking they can
see as time goes on
His unfolding plan.
He puts the desire
for change in their hearts,
but also requires
their flesh to depart.
He wants them to see
that it's only through Him
that an answer to prayer
now can begin.
Jesus once asked the crowd,
"Do you follow Me so
because you want bread,
or My love bestowed?"
Do you ask for your pleasure?

Do you appeal to your need?
Do you seek from desire
that His will succeed?
His will is forgiveness.
His will is to bless.
His will is for healing,
obedience, kindness.
If these are your prayer,
continue to knock,
For it says to "keep asking"
and He will unlock.

Life is...

"For God wanted them to know that the riches and glory of Christ are for you Gentiles, too. And this is the secret: Christ lives in you. This gives you assurance of sharing his glory."
—*Colossians 1:27*

Life is like an apple.
Maybe you have heard.
If you'll listen closely,
it's really not absurd.
When you're young, life's shiny,
like a bright red apple peel.
And it really takes some time
before what's 'neath's revealed.
You chomp and chomp away
to get to what's inside,
like children who are anxious
to see what grown-ups hide.
And once that red peel's broken,
you glimpse the meat within.
The contrast of its whiteness
seems almost amazin'.
You decide you cannot wait
to revel in this delight.
So you plunge your teeth right into
this awe-inspiring sight.
Your taste buds start to work,
as you slosh this bit around.
But to your great amazement,
the white meat's turning brown!

And the taste is not as sweet
as you had first expected.
And because it's somewhat tart,
your hopes become dejected.
But hang in with me now!
This tale's not hardly through.
There's more to life than this.
There's more that you can do.
You do not have to sit here,
hopeless and heartless in mind.
You can open up the Bible
and read Romans 10:9.
If you do what's written there,
you'll see a new perspective.
You'll find a peace within,
which never was expected.
Now you'll read God's Word,
and glean what's hidden there.
You'll have a greater hope,
and joy that's easily shared.
You'll look at this sad world,
knowing a shiny one's waiting.
And your mind is not discouraged.
Your heart's no longer aching.
Life can be like that apple,
shiny and glorious in hue,
because of your new hope,
the reality of "Christ in you!"

A Hand

*"In my distress I cried out to the LORD; yes, I prayed to my God for help.
He heard me from his sanctuary; my cry to him reached his ears."*
—Psalm 18:6

The stormy sea surges
and makes you feel helpless.
You look for a lifeboat,
but not one emerges.
Your hand is now pierced
as you reach for a limb.
You cling to its sharpness
and scream, your voice dimmed.
The water you swallow
is salty and sour.
You try to breathe through it,
while losing all power.
Then you see it beyond you—
a faltering light.
It seems to aim for you,
growing ever more bright.
You see it just forming—
a boat in your sight,
coming now for you,
across the dark night.
Powered by a force,
guided by a beam,
a hand reaches for you,
and you are released!

Bright Night

"Let us go to the sanctuary of the Lord;
let us worship at the footstool of his throne."
—Psalm 132:7

When I was 16, I asked the Lord into my heart on a mountaintop in Colorado, and I began a journey I will never regret...

Sitting in the starlight,
listening for a prayer,
watching in the still night
to see if He is there.
Wondering what He looks like,
and where is His abode.
Does He live beyond the stars,
and is the sun His home?
Does He breathe the air we breathe,
and see us here below?
Does He understand our needs,
as the world turns to and fro?
Does He contemplate our worth,
and does He really care?
Will He come and speak to me,
or sit with me and share?
Sitting in the darkness,
whispering these thoughts,
looking for some light
that would connect the dots,
I was young and novel.
I did not understand.

It was my only wish
that someone take my hand.
Little did I know,
then when life was new,
how much in me would grow,
just what the Lord would do.
He heard my questions then.
He hears them even now,
answering not through men,
but through spirit somehow.
He led me to a place—
a mountain far away.
He showed me then His grace,
and answered me that day.
On another starry night,
like that one years before,
it was dark but full of light,
and He revealed a door.
And then my eyes were opened.
I began to understand
that far beyond my fears
He reached with His strong hand.
He showed me His own home.
We explored a land so rare—
a place where I could roam,
away from the world's cares.

Now we talk and share
'til nothing's left unsaid.
When you're walking with the Lord,
it's to His place you're led.
You're honored and adored.
You assume a different stance.
When you look into His eyes,
you behold His gentle glance.
It'll make you start to cry,
as you relinquish all your stress.
And you start to understand
His love and tenderness.
You begin to rise above.
Your questions seem to cease,
and you realize
just why you are at peace.
You look into His eyes,
and He explains your worth,
and why the stars do shine,

and what is this new birth.
Thank God for my bright night,
when I thought to ask and know!
May you find such a place
and experience your Source!

To Know

"May God give you more and more grace and peace as you grow in your knowledge of God and Jesus our Lord."
—II Peter 1:2

I came to know Your grace
on a mountain far away,
when You hung upon a stake,
with sinners' faults displayed.

They spat into Your face,
while You beside them prayed.
They didn't know Your grace
or see Your worth unveiled.

They didn't know Your name,
the ending of Your tale,
the glory from Your pain,
or how You'd never fail.

Yet they would stand one day,
beholding what You'd made,
and see Your love make way
for anyone who came.

Starry Eyes

"Jesus says, 'I am the light of the world. If you follow me, you won't have to walk in darkness, because you will have the light that leads to life.'"
—John 8:12

There were starry eyes in heaven
when the Lord of Light was born,
and the angels celebrated,
and the once dark night was torn.

As He walked the earth elated
by His Father's will unleashed,
as He talked to temple leaders,
new love words were then released.

As he guided the disciples
through the torrents of a veil,
pointing out the leaders' leaven
with a parable and tale.

As He stepped into the temple,
turning tables of the thieves,
His foot was on their hands
as they tried to take and seize.

As He hung in shame and sorrow
on a tree that others made,
He forgave them for their cruelty,
showed true love instead of hate.

As He rose from caves of darkness,
furling forth a heavy stone,
He released us from our sorrows,
making us as heaven's own.

As He lives and moves within us,
continuing on this earth,
there are starry eyes in heaven,
celebrating His rebirth!

Like Manna

"Jesus said, 'I tell you the truth, Moses didn't give you bread from heaven. My Father did. And now he offers you the true bread from heaven."
—John 6:32

In the pure snowflakes,
a portend I see—
fluffy white manna—
seeds that will feed.
Moistening, grooming
for emergence and growth,
it prepares for a season
not seen yet below.
From death on to life,
we see a green newness.
When once we had suffered,
our lives attain fullness.
With colors abounding
and fragrance unfolding,
we are at once changed,
while You are beholding.

Look into My Eyes

"I pray that your hearts will be flooded with light so that you can understand the confident hope he has given to those he called— his holy people who are his rich and glorious inheritance."
—Ephesians 1:18

When I look into your eyes,
it's shining stars I see,
burning ever brighter
for eternity.

When I look into your heart,
there is a glowing fire
blazing brilliantly.
The flames are rising higher.

When I look into your soul,
I see your love and life.
I see new peace and freedom,
and all release from strife.

Look into My eyes,
as I look into yours.
See My boundless glory
that rushes in and soars.

Spring

"Open up, O heaven, and pour out your righteousness. Let the earth open wide so salvation and righteousness can sprout up together. I, the Lord, created them."
—Isaiah 45:8

Fresh is the air
as springtime approaches.
Sweetly we bear
winter's reproaches.

Cool and crisp breezes
move cloudless skies.
Reactive sneezes
moisten our eyes.

First signs of flowers,
birds in the trees,
green-arching bowers
blossom to please.

Springy grass touches
open-toed shoes.
Picnics and lunches
bring hammocked snoozes.

Radiant sunlight
warms exposed skin.
Taking deep breaths,
we watch life begin.

Make Believe

"All around him was a glowing halo, like a rainbow shining in the clouds on a rainy day. This is what the glory of the LORD looked like to me."
—Ezekiel 1:28

Make believe you are a sunset.
Spread your fingers to the sun.
Paint the sky with all life's colors—
red and yellow, orange and brown.
Touch the treetops with new glory.
Make them glisten. Make them shine.
Make their leaves look phosphorescent
as they float down to the ground.
Put a halo around each mountain
made of small white fluffy clouds.
Let the snowcapped peaks break through
their thin and wispy shrouds.
Reaching up into the heavens,
stretch the clouds with stroking fingers,
making them reflect more colors
for the Son Who sighs and lingers.

Numbered Days

*"LORD, remind me how brief my time on earth will be.
Remind me that my days are numbered—how fleeting my life is."
—Psalm 39:4*

It's not in length of life
that we see great purity.
It's not through numbered days
that rightness is released.

Often the good die young,
while woeful ones remain.
God sees the hearts of men
and how they live, detained.

Some do much in life,
though their days are few and short,
while others live for years,
with little to report.

Our days are numbered so,
not in their multitude,
but in how well we follow
the Lord of Life Who rules.

My All in All

"You must love the Lord your God with all your heart, all your soul, all your mind, and all your strength."
—Mark 12:30

Be my joy as I proceed.
Be my strength in every need.
Be my love that I not grieve.
Be my hope, my light indeed.
Be my wisdom, guiding me.
Be my pleasure that I seek.

All in All, my One True Love,
succoring, strengthening from above,
prepare me for my truest call.
For You are my All in All.

With Your Love

"So God can point to us in all future ages as examples of the incredible wealth of his grace and kindness toward us, as shown in all he has done for us who are united with Christ Jesus."
—*Ephesians 2:7*

With Your joy, hearten me.
With Your strength, lift me.
With Your love, embrace me.
With Your mercy, deliver me.
With Your peace, surround me.
With Your goodness, spare me.
With Your forgiveness, lead me.
With Your gentleness, soften me.
With Your courage, strengthen me.
With Your kindness, encourage me.

A Quiet Sound

"The God of our ancestors has chosen you to know his will and to see the Righteous One and hear him speak."
—Acts 22:14

People announce their coming
with loudness all around—
blazoning manmade objects,
that blast to make a sound.
When Jesus arrives within us,
He brings a voice that's near—
audible, perceived
by those with ears to hear.
In a world full of distractions,
which sound do you choose to hear?
The booming loudness all around,
or a still, small voice so clear?

Whether Whispers

"All who hate me whisper about me, imagining the worst."
—Psalm 41:7

The tethered whispers behind my back
don't hurt me like before,
since I can see Your heart for me
and what You have in store.

Your love and acceptance of who I am,
and Your words of encouragement,
have helped me see and understand
I'm not liable to them.

You taught me and reminded me
and showed me what to do—
that as long as I followed Your ways,
My path would be straight and true.

Whether or not they accept who I am,
agree or care for me,
it doesn't matter at all because
Your love is all I need.

It May Not Be Prudent

*"We are hunted down, but never abandoned by God.
We get knocked down, but we are not destroyed."*
—II Corinthians 4:9

It may not be "prudent,"
to believe as I do.
It may not be trendy.
It may not be cool.

Others may whisper,
and point out my faults,
avoid me altogether,
and use words like, "She's not...."

I may not be party
to fares of desire—
rallies or meetings,
or pastimes admired.

They say I'm a loner.
Not many accept
a lifetime of change,
disdain, and rejection.

In truth, I have peace
and joy without measure,
the love of a Father,
a relationship I treasure.

He speaks to me daily
and guides me with mercy.
He holds and adores me,
and tells me He loves me.

There is not a token
or playbook or treasure
worth what I have in Him—
joy without measure.

Naked

"Let your unfailing love surround us, LORD, for our hope is in you alone."
—Psalm 33:22

Sometimes
we push people
away,
worrying
they may notice
how we're
flawed and imperfect.
We're afraid that,
if they see us as we are,
in our nakedness,
they may find fault,
or reject us,
or speak out against us.

The Lord is teaching me
that He loves me,
no matter what people say,
or how they view me.
He shows me
His mercy, His kindness,
when others are unkind.
He desires for me
a blessing,
when others can't bless.
He teaches me
to love,

when others are past loving.
He reveals to me
that His love abounds
for me,
even when
I feel
unloved or unloveable.

Surround

"How precious is your unfailing love, O God! All humanity finds shelter in the shadow of your wings."
—Psalm 36:7

Lord,
Open to me a day of praise.
Settle my heart with Your love.
Strengthen my hand through prayer-filled days.
Surround me with angels above.

Presence

"Be still in the presence of the LORD, and wait patiently for him to act."
—*Psalm 37:7*

May Your Word be all around me.
May Your love be evident.
May Your peace rest very calmly.
May Your joy be heaven-sent.
May Your life have served a purpose.
May Your memory suffice.
May Your tenderness be in surplus.
May Your heartfelt words entice.
May I ne'er e'er forget You.
May I recognize Your face.
May I see old faith renewing.
May I feel resultant grace.

Give Me a Way

"Teach me your ways, O Lord, that I may live according to your truth!
Grant me purity of heart, so that I may honor you."
—Psalm 86:11

Give me a way
to be closer to You.
Give me a reason,
my Jesus.

Provide me a lesson
and teach me Your ways.
Show me the keys,
my Jesus.

Allow me to view
Your bright-shining face.
Oh, let me see You,
my Jesus.

Walk now beside me.
Lay hold of my hand.
Confirm You are with me,
my Jesus.

Once more as I walk here,
twice more for my joy,
I'll always adore You,
my Jesus.

Go to Arabia

"Nor did I go up to Jerusalem to consult with those who were apostles before I was. Instead, I went away into Arabia, and later I returned to the city of Damascus. Then three years later I went to Jerusalem to get to know Peter, and I stayed with him for fifteen days."
—Galatians 1:17-18

Go to Arabia,
where Paul once went,
bending his knee,
having time spent,
learning to love
Me Who appeared
and interrupted
rebellious years.
Sit still in silence.
Search out My ways.
Listen to hear Me.
Find out what I say.
I'm He Who loves you.
I seek for your soul.
I'm He Who desires
your heart to know.
Come closer to Me
in this busy season.
Spend your time with Me.
Discover the reason.

Tune into My heart.
Experience My words.
Soak in My presence.
Know that you're heard.

How Could I Not?

"My sheep listen to my voice; I know them, and they follow me."
—John 10:27

Your light was so brilliant,
Your scent so divine,
Your treasure so certain,
Your touch so sublime,
Your love was so tender,
Your kindness so rare,
how could I not follow
and go with You there?

Mountains of Grace

*"My heart has heard you say, 'Come and talk with me.'
And my heart responds, 'LORD, I am coming.'"*
—Psalm 27:8

It didn't take long
to recognize Your face,
peering right at me
through mountains of grace.

The blessings You showered,
the rainbow reminders,
the health-saving gestures
among the life-binders.

The dreams now remind me
of Your constant presence,
when all who surround me
seem blind, in remittance.

They shuffle and scurry
until long years late,
then begin to realize
what You meant by a gate.

They come and will come,
though some still deny.
Kind or rude, an awakening
will open their eyes.

In the meantime, in awe,
I sit in Your presence,
as You turn things around
to reveal Your true essence.

The Voice

"Even as he spoke, a bright cloud overshadowed them, and a voice from the cloud said, 'This is my dearly loved Son, who brings me great joy. Listen to him.'"
—Matthew 17:5

The voice unlocks
a rest desired,
a dynamic force,
a passion fired.
a hearty recourse,
a love now known,
a new hope gleaming,
a sure seed sown,
a lingering whisper,
a heartening word,
a rainbow spanning,
a strength enduring,
a sorrow waning,
a cloud to cover,
a warm light shining,
a brand new lover.

What I Love Most

"For his Spirit joins with our spirit to affirm that we are God's children."
—Romans 8:16

What I love most
you may not believe.
It lies in my heart,
in a new place revealed.
Penetrating my soul,
to my mind it gives rest.
Enveloping the whole,
my life it does bless.
With whisperings soft,
it speaks to my ear.
I must listen well,
if I choose to hear.
A silent voice,
but booming and clear,
it speaks to my mind
and makes my eyes tear.
It gives useful words
that answer my needs
and offers assurance.
I'm from my fears freed.
It releases my mind,
and touches my soul,
giving unspoken words
and secrets untold.

You Teach Me

*"'For I know the plans I have for you,' says the LORD.
'They are plans for good and not for disaster,
to give you a future and a hope.'"
—Jeremiah 29:11*

You teach me of wind, sun, and stars,
how light travels swiftly from far,
of pavement with cracks barely seen,
like me, though I'm viewed as a queen,
of Eden, a place You once made—
by Your design it was paved.
Disappointed You must have been,
when Your lovely lady chagrinned.
But You never failed with a plan
of how You would save bitter man.
The course was kept over years,
in spite of our weaknesses, fears.
Each purpose solely was given,
producing bright new stars in heaven.
Now as You teach me my course,
help me to discard remorse.
A pattern is set in my way,
as a new Star lights a new day.

Your Word

"Make them holy by your truth; teach them your word, which is truth."
—John 17:17

Your Word speaks to me
in a thousand different ways.
It gives me direction,
when I am lost.
It gives me hope,
when I'm in despair.
It gives me peace,
when I feel anxious.
It gives me joy,
when I am depressed.
It gives me humility,
when pride vaunts itself.
It shows me kindness,
when I resist reprisal.
It reminds me of Your love,
when I feel deserted.
It brings me back to You,
when I am misled.

Pure Joy

*"I have told you these things so that you will be filled with my joy.
Yes, your joy will overflow!"*
—John 15:11

Oh, the joy to sit and seek You.
Oh, the bliss to be refreshed.
In Your peace to become rested.
In Your presence ever blessed.

Oh, the love—I feel surrounded.
Oh, the warmth that comforts, holds.
In Your kindness never bested.
In Your hands that now enfold.

Oh, the energy injected.
Oh, the liveliness imbued.
In Your armor now I'm suited.
In Your strength I am endued.

Gracious Lord

"You, O Lord, are a God of compassion and mercy, slow to get angry and filled with unfailing love and faithfulness."
—*Psalm 86:15*

Soothing touch,
beyond mercy,
healing hand,
stroking palm.

Warm embrace,
beyond pity,
bringing peace,
loving balm.

Tender words,
beyond insight,
helping sort,
leaving calm.

Gracious Lord,
beyond praises,
lifting up
anointed psalms.

Simple Love

"This hope will not lead to disappointment. For we know how dearly God loves us, because he has given us the Holy Spirit to fill our hearts with his love."
—Romans 5:5

It isn't Your touch
that means so much,
or Your comforting words inspiring.
It isn't Your smile
that often beguiles,
or Your helpful hands untiring.

It's Your love
sent from above
and Your embracing ways fulfilling.
It's Your quiet resolve
to seek and to solve
every prayer request so willingly.

Shudder

"He leads the humble in doing right, teaching them his way."
—Psalm 25:9

I shudder to think of Your mercy,
how You never fail to come through,
when we ask for Your help and forgiveness
for placing ourselves above You.
I shudder to think of Your kindness,
when we often hide from Your face,
thinking it best to forge on,
creating a path our own way.
In humbleness let us beseech You.
In honesty may You prevail.
In heart-reach may we acknowledge
Your hand on our lives availed.

You, Lord

*"'I am the Alpha and the Omega—the beginning and the end,'
says to Lord God. 'I am the one who is, who always was,
and who is still to come—the Almighty One.'"*
—Revelation 1:8

You are awesome.
You are great.
You are ever
and never late.

You are kindness.
You are love.
You give goodness
from above.

You are wonder.
You are might.
You encompass
with pure delight.

You are certain.
You are sure.
You will ever,
and always endure.

I am Yours and You are Mine

"All who are mine belong to you, and you have given them to me, so they bring me glory."
—John 17:10

Lord, You are mine
when spring songs prevail,
when summer sets sail
when fall leaves assail,
when winter winds wail,
Lord, You are mine.

Lord, You are mine
when provisions abound,
when love can be found,
when comfort surrounds,
when all thoughts are sound,
Lord, You are mine.

Lord, I am Yours
when time it does test,
when there is no rest,
when none can attest,
when all peace heads west,
Lord, I am Yours.

Lord, I am Yours
when conflicts arise,
when the deadly despise,
when rumors apprise,
when hatred seems wise,
Lord, I am Yours.

Pitch

"Your royal husband delights in your beauty; honor him, for he is your lord."
—Psalm 45:11

Breathe on me, oh breath of life.
Release me from all fear and strife.
Make me one with You in love.
Touch me, beautiful, heaven-sent Dove.

Show me more of Your delight.
Spread Your wings and give me flight.
Take me with You where'er You go.
Show me wonders here below.

Speak to me in visions, dreams.
Enlighten me with Your radiant beams.
Soar with me through eternity.
Give me strength now to proceed.

Whisper to me words of praise.
Strengthen, lengthen work-filled days.
Remind me of Your presence sure.
Pour Your love that helps endure.

Delights

"Your royal husband delights in your beauty; honor him, for he is your lord."
—*Psalm 45:11*

Breathe on me, oh breath of life.
Release me from all fear and strife.
Make me one with You in love.
Touch me, beautiful, heaven-sent Dove.

Show me more of Your delight.
Spread Your wings and give me flight.
Take me with You where'er You go.
Show me wonders here below.

Speak to me in visions, dreams.
Enlighten me with Your radiant beams.
Soar with me through eternity.
Give me strength now to proceed.

Whisper to me words of praise.
Strengthen, lengthen work-filled days.
Remind me of Your presence sure.
Pour Your love that helps endure.

How Wonderful

"O LORD, I will honor and praise your name, for you are my God. You do such wonderful things! You planned them long ago, and now you have accomplished them."
—Isaiah 25:1

How great is Your faithfulness,
Your ways past finding out.
How wonderful are Your works,
Your beauty that surrounds.
How righteous are Your ways;
we're sufficient on Your path.
How lovely is Your acceptance,
Your mercy and understanding.
How bountiful is Your goodness,
the power of Your hand.
How soothing is Your touch
that brings peace to all our plans.
How much I long to see You
and know You more and more.
How I wish to kneel before You,
to bow to the One I adore.
How grateful I am for Your presence,
Your walk with me up each hill.
How thankful I am for what You've done,
the promises You made and fulfilled.
How magnificent You are,
a great God, worthy of praise.
How wonderful is Your love,
Your awesome, amazing grace.

All These Things

"So if you sinful people know how to give good gifts to your children, how much more will your heavenly Father give good gifts to those who ask him."
—Matthew 7:11

A magnificent sequoia.
A small green leaf.
A pretty purple violet.
A fragrant cup of tea.
Leaves that look like gold
when the sun begins to shine.
A baby to love and hold
and watch grow up with time.
A husband who does love me.
Friends who laugh and sigh.
Granddaughters to rise above me.
Grandsons to enjoy with pride.
All these things He gave me
just because He loves me so.
What a wonderful Friend He is,
still beside me as I grow old.

How He wants to work through you!

Live love, because He loves you so.

"Love each other in the same
way I have loved you."

—JOHN 15:12

My Heart Overflows

"We love each other because he first loved us."
—I John 4:19

My heart overflows
with Your love,
Your kindness to me,
and Your constant reminders
that You are near me.
When others
may not be here,
You are.
Thank You
for being my Friend,
and for sharing
Your love with me.
I see now…
how You are my Lover,
my Friend,
my true Soul Mate.
You are Light and Life,
my Source of joy,
and peace, and hope.
You open doors,
and shut them,
to protect me.
You long,
as I do,
for love
and acceptance.

You give,
and shower me
with kindness.
You pour out
Your blessings
so often
that I can't receive them all.
Help me
to be
what You are
to me
to others.

Will You?

"May God be merciful and bless us. May his face smile with favor on us."
—*Psalm 67:1*

Will You bless this union
made gracious through time,
arranged by Your hand
to reach more by and by?

Will You preserve
my life as I seek
Your wisdom and kindness
in hearts that are meek?

Will You anoint
and extend Your good favor,
as we work together,
adding each our own flavor?

Once

"Heal the sick, and tell them, 'The Kingdom of God is near you now.'"
—Luke 10:9

Tending sheep, He lived His life,
sorting through a world of strife,
opening doors that erst were closed,
clearing paths once overgrown,
healing hearts plugged up with fear,
settling thoughts once in arrears,
striving in His own good way,
bringing light for a new day,
spending time with God alone,
listening to His whispers blown,
leading us in ways laid true,
while bringing others with us too.

A Message of Hope

"In the same way, let your good deeds shine out for all to see, so that everyone will praise your heavenly Father."
—Matthew 5:16

In service He came
and spent His life so,
bringing healing to others
and a message of hope.
When all the naysayers
assaulted and blamed,
He stood for God's purpose—
they were one and the same.
When all the accusers
pointed a finger,
He quietly led others
to God's presence to linger.
His message was simple.
He spoke of God's truth,
not pious sayings,
or laws one must do.
From these He did turn
to reflect something dearer—
God's love to be shared
with those who would hear.

Resurrection

*"Jesus told her, 'I am the resurrection and the life.
Anyone who believes in me will live, even after dying.'"*
—John 11:25

Early morning,
stars above,
glittering embers,
burning love.
Resurrection
from on high,
eliminating
alibis.
Sun revealing
women undone,
crying, asking,
"Where's the Son?"
Angels appearing
in dazzling robes,
standing before them,
questioning, probe.
"Do you seek Him
in a tomb?
He has parted
from this womb.
Go and tell
everyone,
He is risen,
glorified One."
Some will listen.

Some will heed.
Your message given
sows a seed.
Light imparted
causes growth,
resurrection
of seed sown.
Hands uplifted,
hope from above,
glittering embers,
burning love.

On a Beach

"After breakfast Jesus asked Simon Peter, 'Simon, son of John, do you love me more than these?' 'Yes, Lord,' Peter replied, 'you know I love you.' Then feed my lambs,' Jesus told him."
—John 21:15

On a beach by a fire,
You sat and beheld
Your disciples gone fishing,
with stories to tell.
They soon had abandoned
Your work, Your requests,
going back to a job
that was meaningless.
You patiently waited
and called out to them,
"Have you caught any fish?"
You did not condemn.
"Put the net over yonder,"
You said by and by,
and wondered how long before
they'd recognize.
The net soon filled up,
and the fish leapt about.
The disciple You loved most
started to shout.
"It's the Lord!" he exclaimed,
"the One we adore."
They pulled the boat in,
fish and all, to the shore.

Peter jumped first.
He flung on his coat.
He cast down the nets
and sprung from the boat.
They all ran to see You,
crying out with delight.
They had not expected
to behold Your face bright.
They sat alongside You,
and ate and broke bread,
gazing upon You.
Then speaking, You said,
"Simon, do You love Me
much more than these?"
You acknowledged the fish,
of which he was pleased.
"Yes, Lord, you certainly
know that I do."
And he felt convicted
as he turned toward You.
"You must feed My lambs."
Your answer was clear.
You said it again,
two more times sitting there.
"Simon, John's son,
do you really love Me?"
Peter's face sank.
Must he bow to his knees?
"You know that I do,"
he quickly responded.
Could he convince Him
to Whom he was bonded?
"Tend My sheep,"
was again Your reverent plea
to him as he sat,
You said, "Feed My sheep."
"Follow Me" was again
Your lastly request.
And You lingered a little,
but the time was soon past.
These few words You spoke
propelled in their hearts
a ministry to come,
a new life to start.

Many long for You now,
as their lives are undone.
And You beckon us still,
"Feed My sheep, spread My love."
And You sit by a campfire,
beckoning us in
from our boats filled with fish
to a calling within.
And that mission is plain,
never changed over years.
"Tend My sheep, feed My lambs,"
You speak through Your tears.

Fishers

"Jesus called out to them, 'Come, follow me, and I will show you how to fish for people!'"
—Matthew 4:19

Casting our nets
like Fisherman Pete,
for the joy set before us,
when people we reach.
How the angels shout out
when a new one is won
to seek You for glory,
a new life begun.
As fishermen, we
can focus our minds
on sharing and seeking
individuals, all kinds,
to tell them Your story,
to share Your own view,
to witness of glory,
a spirit renewed.

Friend, Ally, and Bro'

"There is no greater love than to lay down one's life for one's friends."
—John 15:13

With pleasantness You offer
Your words of joy and hope,
not infringing on our lives,
until we seek to know.

Gradually it deepens—
a desire to change and grow,
with You as our companion,
friend, ally, and bro'.

We're held inside Your mercy.
Through melting hearts You sow
more seeds of true compassion
inside us here below.

They sprout more fragrant blossoms,
as they begin to grow,
attracting true believers,
formerly unknown.

They seek You with us daily,
desiring with us to know
just how to walk beside You
as friend, ally, and bro'.

Shooting Stars

"The LORD keeps watch over you as you come and go, both now and forever."
—Psalm 121:8

I saw a shooting star near the constellation Orion, and I wondered...

Are our lives like shooting stars,
illuminating the sky briefly,
bringing joy to the onlookers,
who gasp at the wonder
of what we have brought to them—
the love we have offered,
the grace we have portrayed,
the exuberance displayed,
the ways we have changed their lives
by bringing hope and peace,
by explaining Your ways,
and how You are among us
and in us,
and how Your beauty sustains,
and Your brilliance amazes?
Unlike us,
You are constant,
persistent,
lingering,
stable,
like Orion,
year by year
watching over us.

Blaze

*"The way of the righteous is like the first gleam of dawn,
which shines ever brighter until the full light of day."*
—Proverbs 4:18

Today I saw a shooting star. Or was it a firefly?
Whatever it was, I was blessed by its very
bold light in a dark, cloud-filled sky.
It darted across the horizon,
blazing its way with glory,
unaware of the darkness around it,
heedless of the moaning morning.
As creatures stirred and woke to work,
another day newly dawning,
it joyously darted from here to there,
creating a hope-filled awning.
And I thought as I watched, let me do the same,
bringing joy to someone today.
Like the fly or the star, let me blaze a new path,
and create a bright, hope-filled way.

Take Time

"Teach us to realize the brevity of life, so that we may grow in wisdom."
—Psalm 90:12

Will you look with pleasure
on these few earthly days?
Will you begin to treasure
what once seemed like a maze?
Will you wish you'd slowed down
a hurried, busy pace,
to stop and smell the roses,
or on a sunset gaze?
The journey is upon you.
It's what you now do make
that truly shapes the difference
in whatever course you take.
Slow down and look around you,
for your own goodness' sake.
Talk to people near you.
Bring them insight rare.
Your wisdom can inspire,
if you'll take time to share.

Another Day

*"God says, 'At just the right time, I heard you. On the day of salvation, I helped you.'
Indeed, the 'right time' is now. Today is the day of salvation."*
—*II Corinthians 6:2*

Today is another day.
It could be a so-so day,
with nothing too exciting—
everyday events,
meaningless phone calls,
conversations with witless people,
meetings with naysayers.
Or...
It could be disastrous,
where unkind words
bring hateful actions,
and I react
to thoughtless or mean people,
who only have one agenda—
to cause disruption and disaster,
and I fall into these.
Or...
It could be a great day,
a wonder-filled day,
where everything I say
affects lives for good,
bringing them closer to You,
where my words have power,
and my speech speaks
of divine, otherworldly things,

and I see signs and wonders,
and lives are changed
through prayer,
and I draw even closer to You,
and my words bring people to tears,
and to miraculous change,
and I am in the right place
at the right time,
and I see Your hand in it all.

I can choose now.
What sort of day will it be?

Rock My Thoughts

"Let all that I am wait quietly before God, for my hope is in him."
—*Psalm 62:5*

Rock my thoughts.
Steel my soul.
Plant Your love
in me.

Dab my tears.
Heal my heart.
Endure the pain
with me.

Secure my place.
Restore my peace.
Spread Your mercy
through me.

Courage/Persistence

"For I fully expect and hope that I will never be ashamed, but that I will continue to be bold for Christ as I have been in the past. And I trust that my life will bring honor to Christ whether I live or die."
—Philippians 1:20

Lord, I pray for...

courage to reign,
courage to rest,
courage to remain,
with righteousness.

courage to face,
courage to fight,
courage to finish,
with forgiveness.

persistence to move,
persistence to make,
persistence to mold,
with mindfulness.

persistence to sit,
persistence to stand,
persistence to share,
with sourcefulness.

Multiply

"Now may the God of peace make you holy in every way, and may your whole spirit and soul and body be kept blameless until our Lord Jesus Christ comes again."
—I Thessalonians 5:23

Sanctify me with Your purpose.
Rectify me with Your grace.
Specify to me Your promise.
Multiply for me Your peace.

Beautify the saints before You.
Magnify their words of praise.
Fortify their stand in warfare.
Terrify the enemy's gaze.

Amplify our singing voices.
Mortify our fleshly deeds.
Purify our thoughts of evil.
Testify what this world needs.

Simplify for us Your reasons.
Vilify the hurtful plans.
Unify us in Your purpose.
Pacify us in Your hands.

Stabilize me in Your presence.
Tenderize me with Your love.
Energize the spirit within me.
Vitalize me, Holy Dove.

What I Request

"Therefore, since we are surrounded by such a huge crowd of witnesses to the life of faith, let us strip off every weight that slows us down, especially the sin that so easily trips us up. And let us run with endurance the race God has set before us."
—Hebrews 12:1

Dear Lord, my prayer today is for these...

The affirmations of Abraham.
The justice of Joseph.
The meekness of Moses.
The dedication of Deborah.
The strength of Samson.
The reliability of Ruth.
The stability of Samuel.
The devotion of David.
The sagacity of Solomon.
The matchlessness of Matthew.
The ministrations of Mark.
The love of Luke.
The jubilation of John.
The pluckiness of Peter.
The perseverance of Paul.
The temerity of Timothy.
The joy of Jesus.
The forgiveness of the Father.

My True Self

"Just as our bodies have many parts and each part has a special function, so it is with Christ's body. We are many parts of one body, and we all belong to each other."
—Romans 12:4-5

Simply, simply longing
for life, a breath, a change.
For a sense of true belonging,
I will gladly rearrange.

Trying, trying truly
to find my specialty,
thinking it's my duty
to uncover what's beneath.

Clearly, clearly others
see what's evident.
Not hidden or in secret,
they see my one true bent.

Peering, peering closely,
I see it with new eyes.
Like clothes it fits me mostly
when I choose the correct size.

Happily, happily living,
I enjoy my life the best,
when I stir it up with giving,
by using tenderness.

My Harbor

"What a blessing was that stillness as he brought them safely into harbor!"
—Psalm 107:30

Sometimes I feel I've lost it,
as worries seem to mount,
and patience flies away,
and my mind is filled with doubts,
when others do not hear me,
or dismiss me readily,
without an understanding,
having no eyes to see.
Then I again come to You
into our quiet place,
in the corner on the floor,
with a lamp to light the space.
And I reach into my basket
for my Bible and my books,
and I open up the covers,
and I begin to take a look.
And I pour my heart out to You,
because I love You so—
my Redeemer and my Helper,
the Harbor of my soul.
And I give You my frustrations,
unforgiveness, lack of love,
hurtful thoughts, and pounding headache.
I release them with a shove.
And I ask You to be near me.
And I long for Your deep grace.

And I yearn to know Your mercy,
seeking kindness in Your face.
Then I hear Your voice so quiet,
whispering softly in my ear,
and I feel Your strengthening hand,
and I release my inner fears.
As I listen, You encourage,
and You give me sound advice.
And You gradually uncover
a plan for my own life.
You tell me You can help me,
so others I can heal
and bring them closer to You,
and Your plan for them reveal.
I feel Your power in me,
as my mind is now made whole,
and I seek to do Your bidding,
all because I love You so.

A Trainer

*"The LORD directs the steps of the godly.
He delights in every detail of their lives."*
—Psalm 37:23

A trainer, You say,
You'll cause me to teach!
And here I am lacking—
so few I have reached.
But, yes, You have pledged
to make my words great,
as I speak of Your promises
long ago made.
You'll prepare me a place,
set me on high,
let me sit at your feet,
praising You by and by.
Though I do not deserve it—
like Moses, I stutter,
You'll give me the words,
the thoughts I should utter.
I must travel with You,
as You give me speed,
and work Your work through me
to meet every need.
To me You will bring
the people who crave
Your presence, Your mercy,
so souls You can save.

Help Me

"If I gave everything I have to the poor and even sacrificed my body, I could boast about it; but if I didn't love others, I would have gained nothing."
—I Corinthians 13:3

Help me to show mercy,
when others disappoint,
when loved ones seem to falter,
with anger out of joint,
when people who are near me
rush and hurry by,
ignoring my existence,
my whispering heart's cry.

Help me forgive wholly,
when family offends,
when people whom I've cared for
never make amends.
When some are gone and buried,
let me see their face,
fondly to remember
moments of pure grace.

LELE'S SELAH

In my quiet time,
when I settle and reflect,
let me feel Your joy,
Your hope, and Your respect.
Let me know Your peace,
and love those who have come,
remembering how You loved
all in spite of some.

A Prayer

"Devote yourselves to prayer with an alert mind and a thankful heart."
—*Colossians 4:2*

Sisters,
mothers,
fathers, brothers,
friends and lovers,
and many others...
for them I pray
every day.
As oft as I may,
Your words I proclaim
to bring hope and peace,
heart-warming release.
Oh, that they'd return
to Your love that burns,
that their hearts might stir
with spiritual yearning.
Should I forget
to spread Your net,
remind me of my debt
and of my need to beget,
and how they should know
Your great kindnesses shown,
how Your words revealed
can support, help, heal,
restore, bless
and so much
more.

Rocking the Boat

"Jesus replied, 'Who is my mother? Who are my brothers?' Then he looked at those around him and said, 'Look, these are my mother and brothers.'"
—Mark 3:33-34

Remember when I walked
the shores of Galilee?
Remember when I talked
to friends and family?
And often they did question
My true sincerity.
And mostly in their sessions,
they pleaded "peace" with Me.
I must not rock the boat
or cause a mighty stir.
Acclimatize instead,
and follow customs sure.
It wasn't 'til I left—
they saw what I had done,
and they became bereft,
recognizing God's own Son.
But many remained hardened.
Their hearts could not be changed.
They saw themselves in charge
and others as deranged.
You cannot often reach
those who are close to you,
because they want to teach
and maintain their own view.

Seek others whom I bring
and set before your face.
Then praises you will sing
in your new earthly place.

Difficult Children

*"His preaching will turn the hearts of the fathers to their children,
and the hearts of children to their fathers."*
—Malachi 4:6

Children who are easy,
compliant, managed, still,
may not be best in His use,
because they lack the will.
Often the ones who struggle,
causing grief and pain,
are the very ones He's chosen
to reap His worldly gain.
They push and beg for mercy,
and cause upheaval now.
They often lack the graces,
doing what you don't allow.
They go beyond the limits.
They bend the man-made rules.
And, with determination,
are viewed as faulty fools.
But as their lives continue,
God's plan becomes revealed.
It may surprise naysayers
just how He uses zeal.
Imagine how the parents
of Jesus or of Paul
experienced frustration
at their strange heavenly call.
When Jesus wandered off

at the young age of twelve,
were His parents angry that
He'd neglected to tell?
I'm sure that Paul's own parents,
when he began to lead,
were frantic with his change,
and with him would entreat.
So, when you watch your children,
and sigh with patience gone,
open your eyes to His plan,
and let His will be done!

Stone by Stone

"By doing this they will be storing up their treasure as a good foundation for the future so that they may experience true life."
—I Timothy 6:19

How can I do it?
Which way should I go?
Will the currents be high?
Will the waters be low?
If I cross at the river,
will I take the right bridge?
If I climb the tall mountain,
can I reach the high ridge?
If I speedily move,
will hurdles prevail?
If I budge from my groove,
will assaults assail?
Is there something I don't know,
some thing unforeseen?
If I sit long enough,
will I forfeit my dream?

Instead, let me trust,
believe I can do it,
push myself forward,
thrust my way through it.
Rather, let me rustle
a strong bit of muster,
and step by step conquer
this failed filibuster.

Strength does not come
by sitting and waiting,
worrying and sulking,
anticipating.
It comes day by day,
month by month, year by year.
It's a step-by-step process,
unfounded in fear.
Stone by stone it is built,
like a bridge over water.
Each trestle is set
for a son or a daughter.

The bridge is as strong as
the thoughts in your mind.
You can build it or crush it
with each stone in kind.

Bring

"May the God of your father help you; may the Almighty bless you with the blessings of the heavens above, and blessings of the watery depths below, and blessings of the breasts and womb."
—Genesis 49:25

Bring good food
that I may eat,
and wine that refreshes,
savory sweet.
Bring grandchildren
to adore,
a place for them
in Your arms evermore.
Bring great blessings,
bittersweet—
love from a husband,
hands to meet.
Bring good health
and days that soothe,
not just for me,
but for others too.

Gifts

"In his grace, God has given us different gifts for doing certain things well. So if God has given you the ability to prophesy, speak out with as much faith as God has given you."
—Romans 12:6

Lord,
thanks for a legacy
strong and real,
a family with hope,
children with zeal.
Their eyes mostly guided—
Your hands around theirs.
Their feet on paths
lacking despair.
They have such a sense
of calling, as one
who knows a true purpose,
as Your daughter or son.
You have set before them,
in answer to prayer,
amazing gifts cherished,
sacred and rare.
One's a musician;
one is a mother;
another can write;
and one cares for others.
One savors skateboards;
one enjoys games;
one is a reader;

another debates.
All are so different.
And all are so great.
Let all act in love,
removed from all hate.
Let them remember
from where talents come,
and never forget
Your quite-gifted Son.

Little Pilgrim

*"Since he himself has gone through suffering and testing,
he is able to help us when we are being tested."*
—Hebrews 2:18

To many he was nothing,
just a pilgrim, aimless he,
not a boss with eager staffers
for a WiFi company.
On his knees he spent his mornings
in a room with prayer-filled books.
And his days were spent beseeching
and entreating sidewalk crooks.
To a shop he often wandered,
where a quiet owner read,
seeking answers from newspapers
or what commentaries said.
Every day the pilgrim ventured
to a corner of the store,
asking God for His direction
and the words which would implore.
Then, one day, the owner crumpled.
Looking pale, he moaned and sighed.
Telling clients they must leave now,
he, red-faced, began to cry.
When a customer inquired,
"It's my daughter!" he replied.
"If the doctors cannot cure her,
she will die before sunrise!"
Little Pilgrim sat uneasy.

Last to leave, he took his time.
As he neared the shaking owner,
he reached out as he passed by.
In a moment, hand extended,
Pilgrim's eyes the owner read.
And he knew that he must listen
to the words that would be said.
Little Pilgrim then proceeded,
with a wit unprecedented,
to relate his own true story
of a time that he lamented.

He had once enjoyed a daughter.
She had captured his own heart.
Small and dainty, she sat with him,
as he drove both near and far.
Often, they would sing together,
listening to the radio.
Harmonizing every tune,
they put on their own "road show."
Very wise, she often warned him
that his drinking just might kill.
But he laughed and tipped his bottle,
relishing another swill.
Then, one day, he turned a corner.
Blurry-eyed, he could not see
that a truck was heading toward them
from an alley at top speed.
Later on, he woke, disheveled,
in a white hospital bed.
Whispered voices spoke around him,
and he knew that she was dead.
Overcome with grief and sorrow,
he gave up his former life.
Seeking comfort from Another,
he repented of his strife.
Peaceful now, his way was simple.
But he still relived the pain,
when he gazed across the table
for the smile that made his day.

With compassion, and his hand out,
Pilgrim grabbed the owner's shoulder. "He can help you now. Just trust Him.
I can speak now...wiser, older." Then he prayed for the store owner
and his daughter to be healed.
Their hands met across the table,

breaching gaps, their requests sealed.
And they wandered out together,
arm in arm into the night,
the store owner to a bed side,
the small pilgrim to his plight.
Some days later, Pilgrim wondered
how the owner's daughter fared.
So he ventured toward the building,
hesitating, feeling scared.
What if she had not recovered?
What if she had gotten worse?
What if their prayers went unanswered?
What if this was just a curse?
He gazed now into the window
just to see what he could see.
A small girl behind the counter
laughed and giggled happily.
Beside her stood the owner,
his arm around her shoulder.
Looking joyful now and peaceful,
he smiled broadly...wiser, older.

Clouds Dispersed

"When you are praying, first forgive anyone you are holding a grudge against, so that your Father in heaven will forgive your sins, too."
—Mark 11:25

Sacrificed love shoots life to the heart,
as blood sustains the brain.
Unasked for acts of kindness
bring showers like springtime rain.
Words fitly spoken
send sunshine and peace,
like clouds dispersed
by a sudden breeze.
And forgiveness brings favor
and blessings from God,
like children who realize
how much they are sought.

Fellowship

"We proclaim to you what we ourselves have actually seen and heard so that you may have fellowship with us. And our fellowship is with the Father and with his Son, Jesus Christ."
—I John 1:3

When you're lonely, you do focus
on how others do not see,
how the ones that do surround you
are oblivious to your needs.
Looking critically at your own self,
of your separateness you're aware.
And your sadness doubles daily,
not digesting why you're there.
But, in truth, this place was chosen
by a God Who truly cares,
Who is opting for discretion,
and a true kinship to share.
Trying hard to get attention,
swaying focus now to Him,
working now through isolation
to create a bond undimmed.
Lifting up your eyes to lightness,
changing what you truly see,
recognizing His existence,
step by step to His glory,
listening to His words of comfort,
seeing His own gleam of hope,
accepting His bright friendship,
letting Him with you elope,

you run through fields of rapture.
You delight in reverie.
You're immersed now in His presence,
and with new eyes you can see.
As you look up and all around you,
new friends begin to form.
God brings you new companions,
walking with you through the storm.
Side by side you seek His friendship,
and your differences do fall,
because you look upon Him.
He is your all in all.

No Excuse

"You may think you can condemn such people, but you are just as bad, and you have no excuse! When you say they are wicked and should be punished, you are condemning yourself, for you who judge others do these very same things."
—Romans 2:1

I have no excuse
for meanness or spite.
A heart without pity
will not bring respite.
Justification
for wrong done to me
does not now allow
lack of kindness replete.
And foolishness spoken,
or anger ensconced,
does not give me reason
for a hateful response.

Anger

"Human anger does not produce the righteousness God desires."
—James 1:20

Anger comes from pride—
a truly unholy source.
It can take you for a ride,
if you let it run its course.

Purify my thoughts.
Let my motives come from love.
Sanctify my deeds,
that they stem from grace above.

Show me where I lack,
where the little fissures lie.
Patch my latent cracks
with Your salt before I die.

My soul, let it be pure,
and clean, and full of light.
My heart, though it be stained,
be by Your blood made white.

Morning Bliss

*"Listen to my voice in the morning, LORD. Each morning
I bring my requests to you and wait expectantly."*
—Psalm 5:3

Lord, how difficult,
how stressful is this—
to walk a hard road,
after experiencing Your bliss!
Lord, how I savor
my special morning time,
when I can glean Your favor
and Your awesome love sublime.
Lord, only You
understand my heart
and bring me greatest courage,
before the trials start.
Lord, please remind me
of my first light's pleasure,
when I am retested,
sometimes beyond measure.

My Miracle Worker

"They were convinced by the power of miraculous signs and wonders and by the power of God's Spirit...."
—Romans 15:19

You, God, are my miracle worker.
You give me peace when there is none.
You give me hope when all seems gone.
You give me love when I'm undone.
You give me joy when sadness comes.
Order my steps to a more sure way.
Give me direction throughout the day.
Enlighten me so I know what to say.
Help me to act with no delay.
Forgive me for my shortcomings today.

A Wish for You

"For God is the one who provides seed for the farmer and then bread to eat. In the same way, he will provide and increase your resources and then produce a great harvest of generosity in you."
—II Corinthians 9:10

May your years be spread like buttered bread,
and your months with clear direction.
May your weeks be blessed with joyfulness,
and your days with inspiration.
May your hours be filled with one voice still,
and your minutes with momentum.
May your seconds be staid through help and aid,
and your moments with affection.

Favor

"For whoever finds me finds life and receives favor from the Lord."
—*Proverbs 8:35*

The favor of the Lord
rests solidly on those
whose heart in Him does trust,
whose fright is soon deposed,
whose mind avoids the dust,
whose thoughts on Him do rest,
whose actions celebrate
the reality of what is best.

Touch

"He had healed many people that day so all the
sick people eagerly pushed forward to touch him."
—Mark 3:10

Touch is so important.
It relays a sense of peace.
It heals the brokenhearted.
It brings a new release.
It captures distanced souls.
It overcomes disease.
It grants a certain pardon.
It gives us a new means.

Oh, that I would remember
how a touch can so endear.
When I reach out and hug,
I dismantle my own fear!

Sumptuous

"Jesus Christ is the same yesterday, today, and forever."
—*Hebrews 13:8*

Today's a day of blessing,
as I prepare to work,
a day of hope and mercy,
a day of sumptuous worth.

And as I touch each person,
whom God sends on to me,
I'll give a word of wisdom,
I'll speak some prophecy.

The words that I deliver
can change a soulful life,
and give some needed courage,
and freedom from all strife.

Each touch I give in kindness
can soothe their tearful cries,
and rid them of their blindness,
and open once-closed eyes.

Today

"This is the day the Lord has made. We will rejoice and be glad in it."
—*Psalm 118:24*

Lord....
Today, be in my tongue and in my understanding.
Today, let love abound in all of my surroundings.
Today, with each new touch a God-friendship be stirred.
Today, a heartfelt desire for more of You incurred.
Today, direct me toward Your heart in all my thoughts.
Today, give Me great grace to conquer every doubt.

Let Love Reign

"Love is patient and kind. Love is not jealous or boastful or proud or rude.
It does not demand its own way. It is not irritable, and it keeps
no record of being wronged. It does not rejoice about injustice
but rejoices whenever the truth wins out."
—I Corinthians 13:4-6

Today as You lead me,
guide me to truth.
Open my eyes
to Your wisdom too.
Prepare my mouth
to utter Your grace.
Surround my thoughts
with Your kind embrace.
In rightness reveal
to me Your desire.
Let evil be burned
as chaff in Your fire.
Let judgment come down
only from You,
and critics be called
to Your point of view.
Let love reign supreme
in my beating heart,
as my mind seeks Your love,
and my mouth speaks Your art.

You Worked Through Me

"May he equip you with all you need for doing his will. May he produce in you, through the power of Jesus Christ, every good thing that is pleasing to him. All glory to him forever and ever! Amen."
—Hebrews 13:21

You worked through me
to reach a new friend,
who yearns to know You,
and to see Your glory.
Through Your eyes
I saw her great need,
and my heart longed
to see her blessed,
and made whole—
mentally, physically, spiritually.
She followed me
to a house of prayer,
where fire burns in the hearts
of those who lift their hands
in praise to You, Mighty God,
where souls seek after You,
and are willing to die for You,
but choose to live and love through You.
Seeing her need,
prayer warriors stepped forward,
and powerfully envisioned her

in wholeness, having no lack.
Tears were shed,
oh, Beautiful One.
How glorious You are!
She was healed,
and her burden was lifted,
and she gave her cares
to You, Sovereign One.
You took it all,
and now she is free
to live as You desired.
She glows now with joy.
Her peace is evident.
She exudes love,
because she accepted
Your love offered first.

Begun By Your Words

"When we tell you these things, we do not use words that come from human wisdom. Instead, we speak words given to us by the Spirit, using the Spirit's words to explain spiritual truths."
—I Corinthians 2:13

A room without pity.
A hall without care.
A dark, dreary city,
any light seeming rare.
A people once covered
with shame and despair,
where poverty hovered,
and cleanliness was spared.
You entered, a believer,
and brought them new hope—
a chance to receive
the best way to cope.
You spoke about mercy.
You told an old story.
You introduced pity—
of Christ and His glory.
A bright light soon entered
the squalid, sad hovel.
A warm fire burned
where ashes were shoveled.
You saw a new brightness—
a gleam in their eyes.
They walk now in lightness,
with tears and heart sighs.

They have sweet encounters.
Their faith is restored.
And now love resounds
with joy, peace, and more.
Their needs are now heard,
as they turn toward Him,
all begun by your words
spoken kindly to them.

What's in Store

"God is from everlasting to everlasting."
—Psalm 90:2

We start our lives with lists of things,
like many toys or hats or rings.
But as we age and see through time,
we count our blessings as a sign.

And what we know, or think we glean,
becomes a foggy, smudged smokescreen.
The longer we look, attempting to peer,
the shorter the days, the months, the years.

We pace ourselves as days proceed.
To try and lengthen—that's our need.
Until, in a jolt, we comprehend
eternity's just around the bend!

And then, what difference will it make
if he said this or she did take?
And won't it matter greatly more
if I believed in what's in store?

Wellspring

"May the Lord make your love for one another and for all people grow and overflow, just as our love for you overflows."
—I Thessalonians 3:12

Let me be a wellspring,
slowly flowing from below.
Like a fountain spouting water,
let Christ's peace emerge and grow.
As fresh streams that bubble forth,
may Your grace appear and show,
because I know Your mercy
and Your love that overflows.

Should I Stay or Should I Go?

"May he equip you with all you need for doing his will. May he produce in you, through the power of Jesus Christ, every good thing that is pleasing to him. All glory to him forever and ever! Amen."
—Hebrews 13:21

I'm in my little corner,
where all seems safe and sound.
And only TV tells me
what's happening on the ground.

I go to work each day,
expecting what I've known,
praying for my journey,
His blessings on seeds sown.

But then I see the hardship
in areas of the world,
and I wonder and I ponder
if His will to me is furled.

Should I stay here now and help
and feed the ones He sends?
Or is His new desire
to move me and amend?

So I ask You, Lord, to show me.
What would You have me know.
Make Your wishes very clear.
Should I stay or should I go?

Manna

*"I am the true bread that came down from heaven.
Anyone who eats this bread will not die as your ancestors did
(even though they ate the manna) but will live forever."*
—*John 6:58*

Let me be Your manna,
or "life-bread" as You've spoken.
Help me bear their burdens,
when I just want just a token
of time spent by Your side,
listening to Your words,
touching Your white hem,
breathing in Your myrrh.
When all who now surround me
demand so much attention,
help me follow through,
and give with good intention.
Allow me Your great strength
to kindly answer needs,
the patience to endure
grasping, selfish deeds,
the wisdom to dissect
the best use of my time,
so I can soon return
to Your soft side sublime.

Glowing

*"Come, let us worship and bow down.
Let us kneel before the LORD, our Maker!"*
—Psalm 95:6

Glowing may I shine today,
flowing as I stop and pray,
floating on Your "wonder" wings,
emoting Your great love that sings.
Sharing may I heal life's hurts,
daring as I spread Your words,
riding on Your glorious wave,
striding with Your gifts that save.
Spending time as I do now,
bending to Your heart, I bow.

Let Me Be

"There is more than enough room in my Father's home. If this were not so, would I have told you that I am going to prepare a place for you?"
—John 14:2

Let me be Your mansion,
with rooms and rooms to spare,
accommodating others
You bring to join me there.

Let me be a showcase
of hospitality,
of love and gifts eternal,
answering every need.

Let me be a rainbow,
spreading joy replete,
bending with Your grace
over Your mercy seat.

Still Bent

*"Have compassion on me, LORD, for I am weak.
Heal me, LORD, for my bones are in agony."*
—Psalm 6:2

My knee is still bent.
For healing I pray.
A gift heaven-sent
to bless as it may
two souls who do seek
Your hand in their lives.
With hearts that are meek,
they ask to be whole.
They suffer from cancer.
It eats and attacks.
They do seek an answer
to physical lacks.
So to You I come,
with prayers and requests,
as I search Your good book
and await Your bequest.

Special Messengers

*"For we speak as messengers approved by God
to be entrusted with the Good News."*
—1 Thessalonians 2:4

From the book of Acts

Sailing on seas
to places unknown,
they traveled with You,
and leaned on Your grace.
Following Your bidding,
they found those who would
believe and accept,
who desired to know
Who You are,
and how You save
to the uttermost.
They revealed
why You came—
to deliver from fear
and hatred
and death,
and to bring people
new life
and peace.
They spoke
in synagogues
and town squares,
on hills,

and in homes.
They were unafraid
of persecutors
and defamers.
And, because of them,
many were saved,
and came to
a knowledge of truth,
and prayed,
and praised,
and gave thanks.
All because
they were brave
in Your love.

I Want to...

*"Your unfailing love is better than life itself; how I praise you!
I will praise you as long as I live, lifting up my hands to you in prayer."
—Psalm 63:3-4*

I want to worship passionately—
be enamored by Your love.
I want to be amazed
by Your power all around me.
I want to shed all fear
and, in reckless abandon,
follow Your lead.
I want to be free from worry,
and take on every task You ask of me.
I want to be slow to anger,
and see Your goodness
as You work in others' lives too.
I want to be ever patient,
having a long-suffering soul
in every situation.

Give Me Some Guts

"Wake up and look around. The fields are already ripe for harvest."
—John 4:35

Give me some guts, Lord,
so I may serve,
standing so firm,
with no fear, undisturbed.

Give me a sword, Lord,
shaped from Your gold,
so I won't waiver
from Your will bestowed.

Give me a torchlight
of Your own bright brass
to guide and direct me,
like the sail on a mast.

Give me Your heart, Lord,
of unswerving belief,
so I may venture
through white fields replete.

Facing My Foes

*"Be strong and courageous! Don't be afraid or discouraged...
for there is a power far greater on our side!"*
—II Chronicles 32:7

Lord...
Give me courage to face my foes
and many of my friends!
Give me wisdom to speak your words.
May Your insight never end!
Give me freedom undaunted by fear,
courage Your path to tread.
Give me life for as long as You need me
to walk among the dead.

Renew

"He fills my life with good things. My youth is renewed like the eagle's!"
—Psalm 103:5

Renew your mind
by donning My thoughts.
Renew your strength
by listening to My words daily.
Renew your peace
by focusing on the words I give you.
Renew your joy,
by experiencing the rejoicing of fellowship with Me.
Renew your love for others
by centering your actions on what you have learned from Me.

Remember My Love

*"God showed his great love for us by sending
Christ to die for us while we were still sinners."*
—Romans 5:8

Remember My love
when you are down,
when you feel discouraged
and embraced by a frown.

Remember My power
when you are afraid.
Remember My Son,
and all that He gave.

With Me you are free
to live and to love.
And to share My good message
of words from above.

With Me you can be
a spiritual being,
walking with angels,
completely set free.

Because

*"'The message is very close at hand; it is on your lips and in your heart.'
And that message is the very message about faith that we preach."*
—Romans 10:8

Place your heart in My hands.
Place your cares at My feet.
Let My peace prevail in you.

I'll take care of you today.
So don't fear or worry about things to come.
I'm by your side, always guarding and protecting you.

You are blessed,
and you can encourage others.
You can bring them peace and comfort by using the words I give you.

Minister

"The Holy Spirit produces this kind of fruit in our lives: love, joy, peace, patience, kindness, goodness, faithfulness, gentleness, and self-control. There is no law against these things!"
—Galatians 5:22-23

Minister My joy.
Minister My love.
Minister My peace.
Minister My patience.
Minister My goodness.
Minister My meekness.
Minister My gentleness.
Minister My faithfulness.
Minister My self-control.

His Lamp

"You are the light of the world—like a city on a hilltop that cannot be hidden. No one lights a lamp and then puts it under a basket. Instead, a lamp is placed on a stand, where it gives light to everyone in the house. In the same way, let your good deeds shine our for all to see, so that everyone will praise your heavenly Father."
—Matthew 5:14-16

Your feet walk in My path.
Your eyes see what I reveal.
Your hands offer My mercy.
Your peace is My gift to you.
Your healing is in My hands.
Your voice carries My words.
Your lips pronounce My love.
Your strength comes from Me.
Your love emanates from Mine.
Your heart releases My tenderness.

Walk with Me.
Seek My joy.
Seek My love.
Seek My peace.
Seek My mercy.
Seek My power.
Seek My healing.
Seek My kindness.
Seek My tenderness.
Speak My Word.
Shine My light.

Adamant

"The people...won't listen to you any more than they listen to me! For the whole lot of them are hard-hearted and stubborn. But look, I have made you as obstinate and hard-hearted as they are. I have made your forehead as hard as the hardest rock! So don't be afraid of them or fear their angry looks, even though they are rebels."
—Ezekiel 3:7-9

You are like a diamond,
forever "forehead strong."
He said, "By the people
is where you belong.
Your belief is dedicated
against the froward faces.
Like the adamant you're tough,
set firm in all your places.
Never be afraid,
when they balk and talk against you.
It's Me they come against
and devotion to My view.
They often will not listen,
or take note of what you say.
But, be stalwart as a rock,
imperious in that day.
Daughter, you must always
hear the words I speak
into your heart and ears,
and invariably stay meek!

They may move away,
be unwilling to repent.
But I will stand beside you,
unrelenting, adamant."

Women, Take Up Your Swords!

"Take the sword of the Spirit, which is the word of God."
—Ephesians 6:17

Deborah did it.
Abigail too.
Ruth also held to
His words of truth.

Mary was awestruck,
a little afraid,
but her belief
bade her obey.

Huldah recited
His words to change.
Hannah prayed openly,
although she seemed strange.

Esther was called to
a sovereign life.
It was her words that
cut through the strife.

All of these women
could have slept,
leaving neglected
a world bereft.

But they showed bravery,
believing their Master,
and, with His guidance,
avoided disaster.

Can we now listen?
Can we be brave?
What royal message
leads us to save?

Put on your armor.
Take up His sword.
With Him by your side,
you'll never be bored!

Our Defense

*"Put on all God's armor so that you will be able to
stand firm against the strategies of the devil."*
—*Ephesians 6:11*

Our defense is not with weapons
carved from wood, or stone, or steel.
Our defense is not with castles
built with buttresses real.
We defend ourselves with armor
forged from spiritual descent.
And although it can't be seen,
it's the surest armament.
For we wrestle not with flesh,
nor against the reddest blood.
Our attacks cannot be seen,
though they hit us like a flood.
Our attacker has a plan,
with his cunning art defined.
We must know his stratagem
and the pattern of his lies.
He is ruler of all darkness.
He has wickedness, deceit.
He attacks with accusations
and arranges trickery.
He can scare and paralyze us,
if we do not know our place.
He can cover up his plan,
if we do not see his face.
We must understand his ways.

We must know our true defense.
Putting on our true armor,
we can win the fight needless.
Knowing truth protects our thoughts—
that's the belt around our loins.
And right standing with our God
is the breastplate that adjoins.
Prepared, our feet are shod
with His own gospel of peace.
Saving faith is what protects
from his missiles, like a shield.
And salvation we do wear
like a helmet on our head.
God's Word is what we wield
like a sword to conquer death.
Praying always to that end,
in the spirit, with entreaty.
With alertness, perseverance,
we will win and soon defeat him.

Sing a Song

"Sing to him; yes, sing his praises. Tell everyone about his wonderful deeds."
—*I Chronicles 16:9*

Sing a song of blessing.
Sing a song of praise.
Sing a song, a message,
of what the Lord has made.
Make it ever joyful,
full of love and light.
Make it ever peaceful,
shaping what is right.
Sing a song of glory,
of Jesus, God's own Son.
Bring us a new story
of all the souls you've won.
Sing as you go forward
to work or play or fun.
Sing as you are happy
for what the Lord has done.

Praise God

"Let everything that breathes sing praises to the LORD! Praise the LORD!"
—*Psalm 150:6*

Praise God today and every day.
Praise Him from Whom all blessings flow.
Praise Him for His great wisdom, love, and peace.
Praise Him for His matchless gift—His Word.
Magnify His Word and thank Him for it.
Like a fountain, it flows down
grace and mercy to us.
It lifts us up to the sky,
so far above the earth.

Praise God for His mighty works
and for His benefits to us who believe.
Laud Him and thank Him and glorify Him,
for He made us and He gave us all that we have.
Praise Him for His love and His kindness toward us,
which He freely gives to us each moment of every day.

Praise God for His mercy, which He abounds toward us.
Praise Him for His continuous grace, His divine favor,
which He showers on us throughout our lives,
even when we are the most undeserving.
Praise Him through your thoughts,
through your body, your spirit.
Praise Him today,
and every day.
Selah.

Christmas Eve Praise

*"All praise to God, the Father of our Lord Jesus Christ.
God is our merciful Father and the source of all comfort."
—II Corinthians 1:3*

I praise You on this eve,
when silence is my guest,
and stars cover the skies,
and many take their rest.

I look to You and trust You,
when others watch with fear,
and count the days and hours,
and grit their teeth and peer.

I behold Your face with peace,
when others sadly fill
and drive their days through work,
and are most anxious still.

I see You in the stillness,
when others joke and jest,
and play their mindless games,
and wonder what is next.

I greet Your words with joy,
when others are quite sad,
and dote on misery,
and how can they be glad?

I love You in the midst,
when some things aren't quite right,
and You reach out Your hand,
and demonstrate Your might.

A Soldier's Byway

"You must each decide in your heart how much to give. And don't give reluctantly or in response to pressure. 'For God loves a person who gives cheerfully.'"
—II Corinthians 9:7

As you sail along life's byway,
when once you service-cruised,
just remember how your efforts
and your deeds helped others choose.

Your example was a good one.
Your life, it really shone.
And you took the time to defend
the rights that others won.

Thank you for your service.
May it return to you in spades.
You are a great success,
because you forward paid.

Thanks

"I know all the things you do. I have seen your love, your faith, your service, and your patient endurance. And I can see your constant improvement in all these things."
—Revelation 2:19

Words expressed
are meaningless,
unless they're charged
with fruitfulness.

Thanks for all that you have done,
for all the service you've begun,
for deeds that bring a sense of peace,
because you fought and finally won.

How He longs to live with you forever!

Watch for Him, because He will come for you....

"Behold, He is coming with the clouds,
and every eye will see Him...."
—REVELATION 1:7

The Choice

"You can enter God's Kingdom only through the narrow gate. The highway to hell is broad, and its gate is wide for the many who choose that way. But the gateway to life is very narrow and the road is difficult, and only a few ever find it."
—Matthew 7:13-14

Heaven and hell
are determined by heart.
My sheep hear My voice
and follow afar.
Closeness is governed
by decisions made
and willingness to submit to
a heartfelt embrace.
It's all very simple,
not complex or clouded.
I give in My mercy
a way free from doubt.
Those who choose to defend
My clear enemy,
in darkness displace Me
eternally.
They decide between light
and a dark way to go.
I beckon so often,
but they resolve so.
Your prayers and beseeching
avail for this life.
Keep up with persistence,
so your choice can be right.

What's in Store

"Store your treasure in heaven, where moths and rust cannot destroy, and thieves do not break in and steal."
—Matthew 6:20

We start our lives with lists of things,
like many cars or trips or rings.
But as we age and see through time,
we count our blessings as a sign.

And what we know, or think we glean,
becomes a foggy, smudged smokescreen.
The longer we look, attempting to peer,
the shorter the days, the months, the years.

We pace ourselves as days proceed.
To try to lengthen—that's our need.
Until, in a jolt, we comprehend
eternity is around the bend!

And then, what difference will it make
if he said this or she did take?
And won't it matter greatly more
if I believed in what's in store?

Go Ahead

"You can make many plans, but the LORD's purpose will prevail."
—Proverbs 19:21

Go ahead with your plans
that don't include Me.
Take your trips.
Make your calls.
Let your speech disagree.

I will work it all out.
I will thwart those who go
behind backs,
telling lies.
In the end I will show.

Then I'll smoothly prevail—
implement with quick speed
My desire,
My will,
and a plan that meets needs.

You Instead

*"I am leaving you with a gift—peace of mind and heart.
And the peace I give is a gift the world cannot give. So don't be troubled or afraid."*
—John 14:27

Today I feel frustration
as the things of man do fail,
trying to work on my computer,
and to read all my email.
It's locked up; I have no access,
and I cannot see my files.
I am urgent to release them,
having deadlines, work-sent trials!
Oh, I long to be in heaven,
where Your peace can finally reign.
There I'll sit with You in pleasure,
where things can't make me insane.
Oh, to luxuriate in Your presence,
far away from man-made things,
looking up into Your visage,
with the joy that Your love brings.
Today on earth release me
from these cares that burden me.
Take me with You to Your glory,
that Your image I may see.
When I look at my computer,
let me glimpse You in its place.
Then Your peace I'll finally feel,
as I look into Your face.

Lamb's Eyes

"The Lamb on the throne will be their Shepherd. He will lead them to springs of life-giving water. And God will wipe every tear from their eyes."
—Revelation 7:17

It doesn't matter how you feel,
My promises are alive.
Whether or not you think I'm real,
I lived, I spoke, I died.
On a mountaintop I taught,
whether you think it's true.
I gave lessons from a Book,
and subverted hate so cruel.
You may turn a cold, blind eye
to all I've said and done,
but one day you will come to see
the City I've begun.
And as you touch the pearly gates,
and see the glassy streets,
you'll be blinded by the gold
and glistening gems replete.
And as you come up to the throne,
My Father you will see,
and the bright eyes of a Lamb,
Who much resembles Me.
There you'll finally come to know
all that you could have been,
but it really is not too late
to decide to enter in.
Come to view my single room,

My furniture adorned.
Sit and bask in pure delight,
and feel a new love born.
See My Lamb's eyes gazing now,
always right here in view.
Come to know My caring stare,
how I've always sought for you.

Sparkle, Shine, and Glow!

"Now may the LORD value my life, even as I have valued yours today. May he rescue me from all my troubles."
—I Samuel 26:24

What if people do not value
or see you for who you are?
What if they just ignore you,
or squint like you're somewhat ajar?
What if they push you aside,
or bully you with their words?
What if they call you names,
or treat you like you're absurd?

It doesn't matter, really.
Who cares if their actions hurt,
when you know in your heart who you are,
when you understand your worth?
How important it is to see clearly!
How important it is to know
that you were once created
to sparkle and shine and glow!

Yes, you were meant for glory,
to live among the stars.
And you were made to be seen,
acknowledged from afar.
So never lose sight of your meaning!
Never forget your name!
How important is your true purpose—
to grasp His offered claim!

Early Morning

*"I long for the Lord more than sentries long for the dawn,
yes, more than sentries long for the dawn."*
—Psalm 130:6

Early morning,
day at dawn,
watched the sunrise,
prayed a psalm.
Saw Your glory
in the clouds
and Your light-filled,
heaven-bound shrouds.
One lone bird
flew above.
Your own creation
speaks of love.
Its shadow reflects
on water below
and shows the mercy
You often sow
in places least thought of,
in people unknown,
in sorrows that turn
Your love to bestow.
The lake was subzero,
but geese calmly swam.
The boats in their places
'til March, like a lamb,

would engender a sunrise,
much like today,
and warmth out of coldness
would melt all away.

The Other Side

"Dear friends, don't be surprised at the fiery trials you are going through, as if something strange were happening to you. Instead, be very glad—for these trials make you partners with Christ in his suffering, so that you will have the onderful joy of seeing his glory when it is revealed to all the world."
—I Peter 4:12-13

Sometimes I encounter
a thing of dread—
an event or a person
to whom I am led.
It's then that I think of
what lies ahead.
If I could just have life
there instead!
You may feel the same
along your way,
encountering hard things,
and times of pain.
And you think if you can just
maintain your stride,
you'll be fine when you reach
the other side.
Life in this world
is the same for us all.
It's hard, that's for sure,
full of heartache and falls.

And what gets us through
this bumpy night ride
is knowing what waits
on the other side.

Red and Bright

*"The people who walk in darkness will see a great light.
For those who live in a land of deep darkness,
a light will shine."*
—Isaiah 9:2

As I walked this morning,
You showed me a bright star,
large and red,
shining in the southeast,
below the moon.
It was larger than
any star
I'd ever seen.
It hung there,
in front of me,
and I watched it,
amazed.
I wondered why
I'd never seen it before.
Then, I became distracted.
I saw a fawn
crossing the road.
And a heron loomed
along the lake beside me.
When I looked up again,
the star was gone.
I looked twice,
three, four times.
It was not there.

And I wondered
what it meant.
I asked You,
and You said,
It represents My presence,
My power in your life.
You are a prayer warrior,
and I work through you
to help others
overcome.
Use this power
wisely.
A great light,
red and bright,
shines from you.
It reminds you
that I will return
for you one day,
as a fiery light,
red and bright.

Your Leading

"Where does light come from, and where does darkness go?"
—Job 38:19

Precious One, You see me here,
and You hear my voice,
asking help in all I do
and direction with each choice.

I am certain of Your presence.
Your words are way more clear,
since I've journeyed now beside You
all these many months and years.

I listen for Your leading,
as each new choice arises,
for an enemy always lurks
in suitable disguises.

I can trust You as my Savior,
as I walk upon this road,
because You strode this path before
and foresaw each pothole.

It was You Who shared Your love,
when others spat, appalled.
Through the torment You considered
the ones who'd hear Your call.

Guide me now as I examine
a fork in this wide road.
Lead me forward once again
to Your peaceable abode.

How Deep?

"God is so rich in mercy, and he loved us so much, that even though we were dead because of our sins, he gave us life when he raised Christ from the dead. (It is only by God's grace that you have been saved!)"
—Ephesians 2:4-5

How deep is Your mercy?
How wide is Your love?
How long is Your patience,
Holy Spirit above?

How terrible the ravage?
How torrential the storm?
How monumental the earthquake
before You return?

We long for Your presence.
We thirst for Your touch.
We crave Your anointing.
We love You so much.

Remind us to seek You.
Remember us now.
Relinquish Your Spirit,
as we worship and bow.

Only You are forever.
Only You are adored.
Only You are most blessed,
equipped, and adorned.

Help us to be like You,
ever filled with Your love.
Help us to pursue You,
As our source from above.

Amazed

"For all that is secret will eventually be brought into the open, and everything that is concealed will be brought to light and made known to all."
—Luke 8:17

Tracing a pattern,
surrounded by grace,
sensing Your vision,
seeking Your face,
clawing to rise up
to that special place,
seeking Your mercy
to see with Your gaze,
knowing within me
of Your special place,
but feeling quite lost
in a whirlwind of haze.
Seeing Your hand
of forgiveness, amazed,
awakened by dreams,
fire-filled earthly spaces.
Within me I'm stirred,
but my vision is dazed.
Lord, help me to see you—
My blindness abates.
Please take my small hand.
Lead me to Your gates—
Your kingdom of kindness,
Your heartfelt embrace.
I will seek You early.

I desire Your reign.
Please lift me up to You.
Let me of You taste.
Forgive my departures,
my actions in haste.
Forgive my impatience
to finish this race.
In silence I seek You—
before You abased.
May I ever adore You,
by Your glory amazed,
in Your plan for me humbled,
as I stand in Your place.
And You reveal Your throne to me—
gem-filled, diamond-laced.

Capture My Heart

"The LORD is my strength and shield. I trust him with all my heart. He helps me, and my heart is filled with joy. I burst out in songs of thanksgiving."
—Psalm 28:7

Surround me with Your cape of kindness.
Capture my heart with Your love.
Mirror my longings to see You.
Envelop my soul with Your glove.
Escape with me to Your abiding.
Run with me to Your lair.
Sustain me on Your food of goodness.
Embrace me with Your arms so fair.

Astounding

*"They were singing the song of Moses, the servant of God, and the song of the Lamb:
"Great and marvelous are your works, O Lord God, the Almighty.
Just and true are your ways, O King of the nations."
—Revelation 15:3*

Amazing Your love,
and all that is in it.
Extraordinary Your grace,
without any limit,
inspiring the trust
that brings us results,
astounding our hearts,
freeing from all lusts.
Sublime Your wisdom
and peacefully serene.
Terrible the outcome,
when we don't believe.
Refreshing the life,
when our flesh is dead.
Exhilarating the hope
that lies ahead.

Glimpses

"The heavens proclaim the glory of God. The skies display his craftsmanship."
—*Psalm 19:1*

You put me in places,
and add to my story,
circling me with views—
glimpses of Your glory.

You place me on cliffs,
overlooking green dales,
with ships passing by
on seas with full sails.

You take me to mountains
and forests with trees—
remote, distant places
to show me Your zeal.

You lead me to beaches—
islands far away—
to reveal Your full glory
and see what You've made.

And I wonder and ponder
what will it be like
when You unveil Your creation—
Your bounty and might!

Honored

*"Look, I am coming soon, bringing my reward with me
to repay all people according to their deeds."*
—*Revelation 22:12*

When people are dishonest,
they attain immediate gain,
but they fail to see the fullness—
the cause of their own bane.
All they see is what's before them—
a way in, a smile, a coin,
a reward for their deception—
food to eat now and enjoy.
What they do not understand
is that they have just now laid
a brick toward their destruction,
not a path that's golden paved.
It's a course that will be balanced
in God's truthful weights and scales,
while it's true worth is determined
by the price that must be paid.
They will answer for injustice
in the end, the final day.
Before Christ they'll bow and answer.
Before Him they must then say
just why their need so urgent
was worth this short-lived sin,
when trust was really needed
and silent prayer to Him.
We are often so confronted

with decisions, good or bad.
It's in these little choices
that our outcome will be had.
We may be going to heaven
and have eternity,
but will we sit beside Him,
or endure another seat?
I want to be up front,
and see His glorious face.
I want to view His smile,
and feel His full embrace,
and know that He is proud
of all that I have done,
and shine with Him in glory,
and be His honored son.

I Have Heard

"So all of us who have had that veil removed can see and reflect the glory of the Lord. And the Lord—who is the Spirit—makes us more and more like him as we are changed into his glorious image."
—II Corinthians 3:18

What have I to give,
when all has been given?
And what can I spare,
when nothing's forgiven?

And how shall I live,
when none can beget,
in a world of great hardship,
sorrows and regrets?

Oh, frivolous world!
Oh, world so unsound!
Oh, world where a tear
falls dry to the ground.

Where dawn rises high
on an earth unprepared,
and smoke blows and coats
all the greenery there.

Where people accuse,
making falseness seem real.
Where sons are dispatched
by lurid appeals.

Where dads disappear,
making bars their abiding,
whitewashing their guilt,
while they are in hiding.

Oh, world without mercy,
oh, darkening night,
where shines the blue sky
or brightness of light?

When stars seem to pierce
and correct with sharp hues,
when comes the Priest-Warrior
to reveal the plain truth?

Climb for me a mountain.
Cross for me the sea.
Walk with me through deserts,
leaving prints to see.

Lead me to Your trueness.
Crown me with delight.
Come for me with newness.
Save me from my plight.

I have heard of Your glory,
how You fought a good fight,
how You embraced all the guilty,
and then how You cried.

I have sensed Your deep presence.
I have whispered soft praise.
I have noticed Your countenance,
smiling brightly through haze.

Can You tell me my name?
Can You make clean my heart?
Can You enter through pain?
Can You form light from dark?

I gasp as I tread.
I look all around.
I hear Your faint footsteps
as they fall to the ground.

Lead me to paths precious,
to innocence there,
where clouds seem to part,
revealing clean air.

Take me up to You now,
away from this world,
where hearts know no pity,
and evil deeds swirl.

I hear Your name, Jesus.
I feel Your strong hand,
as You pull me from drowning
in gripping quicksand.

You engulf me with kindness.
You surround me with peace.
You bless me with freedom.
Your joys never cease.

As I forgive people,
and reach out my hand,
I pull others with me
into Your strong band.

The circle grows larger,
as new ones believe,
and we form an army
that's spiritually conceived.

Your mercy encompasses.
Your love, it enfolds.
Your compassion endures.
Your story unfolds.

In newness we shiver,
shedding old skin,
becoming more like You,
created within.

With armor we rise up,
and reign in Your world.
The darkness disperses.
The evil unfurls.

And we live forever.
By Your side we stand,
in glory abiding
with You, hand in hand.

No Regrets

"For the kind of sorrow God wants us to experience leads us away from sin and results in salvation. There's no regret for that kind of sorrow. But worldly sorrow, which lacks repentance, results in spiritual death."
—II Corinthians 7:10

Your time quickly comes—
of events You have spoken.
I see how the world
is blind to this token.
Your Word clearly shows
the sequence, the pattern,
but many don't see,
not desiring what matters.
Allow testimony—
a witness that's real,
that many may wake up
and take on new zeal.
For You we must live
and, breathing, now speak,
so our lives can resemble
the witnesses You seek.
Then with boldness we'll stand
and warn all the others,
creating a host
of sisters and brothers.
We'll be a great army
of spiritual warriors,
destroying the enemy,

removing the barriers.
As we enter a new realm—
a land everlasting—
no regrets crush as we're
praying and fasting.

The Planets Aligned

"Now all glory to God, who is able to keep you from falling away and will bring you with great joy into his glorious presence without a single fault."
—Jude 1:24

The planets aligned
in threes recently,
and I was reminded
that three means complete.
I wondered and pondered
just what it all means.
Is Your imminent return
coming more suddenly?
Will You welcome us soon,
stand with us face to face,
as we tell all our stories,
how we ran in this race?
And my heart began beating
much faster, it seems,
as I'd seen Your bright presence
in so many dreams.
Would I bow down in awe?
Would I cry with delight?
Would I reach out my hand,
be amazed at the sight?
Would I tell You my story
and be proud of the ending,
how I'd lived out my life
in reverence, bending?
Or would I with deep shame

behold my past,
how I'd continued to sin,
forgetting the last?
Oh, that with honor
I would stand before You,
relating with pleasure
a life love-imbued!

Orion

"It is the LORD who created the stars, the Pleiades and Orion. He turns darkness into morning and day into night. He draws up water from the oceans and pours it down as rain on the land. The LORD is his name!"
—Amos 5:8

Speak to me clearly.
When will You return?
Is the time drawing near
for our old world to burn?

Can our deeds withstand it—
the heat of Your words?
Will Your stance demand it—
preeminence sure?

I see in the stars
Your humbling approach,
when concrete and bars
won't dare to encroach.

You showed me today
what Orion means,
from the stars' bright display—
an upcoming season.

Betelgeuz means "the coming,"
Rigel—"crushing foot,"
Bellatrix—"swift destroying."
How can we but look?

Before my eyes shining—
"light bearing forth,"
as I remain dining
at Your heaven-bound door.

Prepare my heart swiftly
for Your coming day.
Arm me now deftly,
with Your bold array.

May I be prepared
to fight and to stand,
unafraid and daring
to proclaim You at hand.

Arm in Arm

"There will be strange signs in the sun, moon, and stars. And here on earth the nations will be in turmoil, perplexed by the roaring seas and strange tides. People will be terrified at what they see coming upon the earth, for the powers in the heavens will be shaken."
—Luke 21:25-26

Will it be a surprise,
when You return?
Can we ever surmise
the end of our yearning?

Will events come and go,
and we never learn?
What has been foretold,
can we discern?

Are these current events
signs of the times?
Can we tell what You meant?
Is this message mine?

Lord, reveal to me now
what I need to know.
Must I withhold my bow
as "unity" grows?

Must I sternly say no
to pressure revealed?
By Your words that I sow
will my future be sealed?

With step by step show me
the true course to take.
With truth unveiled deftly,
right choices to make.

I trust in You solely,
as options deflect,
and saints stand up boldly,
arm in arm, neck to neck.

Fearless

"This is my command—be strong and courageous! Do not be afraid or discouraged. For the LORD your God is with you wherever you go."
—*Joshua 1:9*

Help me blaze a way
where others dare not tread.
Help me pave a path
that leads to lands of dread.
Help me fearless be
what's needed in that day.
Help me clearly see
what's hidden 'neath the fray.
Help me courageously walk
around this fear-lined space.
Help me always stand,
surrounded by Your grace.

Prepare

"*For you are my hiding place; you protect me from trouble.
You surround me with songs of victory.*"
—*Psalm 32:7*

Prepare us for what lies ahead.
Show us what we must do and how.
Strengthen us with Your armor.
Surround us with Your peace.
Lift us up with Your joy.
Cover us with Your mercy.
Embrace us with Your grace.
Lavish us with Your love.
Be near us as we get closer to the end.

Surely

*"Indeed, the Sovereign LORD never does anything
until he reveals his plans to his servants the prophets."
—Amos 3:7*

Surely You would tell me
before I reach a cliff
and narrowly escape
a fall to an abyss.

Surely You would warn me
before the evil comes,
and I am set for ruin
among Your chosen ones.

Surely You would whisper,
and give me a sure sign—
something unmistaken
to show a way sublime.

Wouldn't it behoove You
to save Your own elect,
and honor them with glory,
and prove they were select?

Your ways are far above me.
Your manners are obscure.
I only know that some day
You'll show me what is sure.

When

*"When the godly are in authority, the people rejoice.
But when the wicked are in power, they groan."*
—Proverbs 29:2

Dear Lord, will You please say
when You will come again?
I look for You each day,
and seek You in the din.
And as the morning breaks,
and light-filled life begins,
I seek You in the fray,
and wonder where You've been.
Is Your heart often swayed?
Are You anxious within?
Are You irritated
by all the worldly spin?
I imagine You're irate—
I am so sure of it—
to look down on such hate,
and not a little bit.
Please make me now aware—
when will You come again?
Then I can easily share
with other women, men.
And make them more aware
of Your unfolding plan.
And help them to prepare
for new life to begin.

Come with Hope

*"I know the LORD is always with me. I will not be shaken,
for he is right beside me."*
—Psalm 16:8

As the days grow shorter, fewer,
and the temperatures arise,
and the enemies' loud voices
threaten war for our demise.
As the missiles grow in number,
and the bombs are built with glee,
out of hatred they are growing
to encumber you and me.
Let my heart remain courageous,
softened still by Your sweet touch.
Let my joy remain undaunted,
through a wellspring, a swift rush.
Give me courage, fearless treasure.
Give me rightful faith in You.
Give me strength beyond all measure—
solidarity that's true.
Stand beside me when clouds thicken,
and the stars fall 'round me here.
When earthquakes shake the planet,
come with hope, uplifting cheer!

War

"*No, despite all these things, overwhelming victory is ours through Christ, who loved us.*"
—Romans 8:37

It is in war
that many have seen
the scourge of the world,
the pleas of the weak.
It is in battle
that all of us see
what we are made of
ultimately.
Day by day,
week by week,
a war wages on,
to many unseen,
while all of us seek
a sure paradise,
where we can be free.
We are plagued in our minds
by a sure enemy,
who entraps and ensnares,
steals, kills, and destroys,
as You prepare
for a certain return.
And while we await,
our only recourse
is to resist the bait,
and its evil source.

By changing our thoughts.
through reliance on You,
and all You have sought,
we can win this war,
and Eden achieve,
and finally, one day,
be physically relieved.
When He comes back for us,
and takes us with Him,
we can live in a world
where all of us win!

The Cherubim

"They were calling out to each other, 'Holy, holy, holy is the LORD of Heaven's Armies! The whole earth is filled with his glory!'"
—Isaiah 6:3

Cherubim aren't angels.
They guard the mercy seat.
In Eden they protected
the Tree of Life replete.
Forever they do bow
as four before the seat,
guarding and protecting
God's vow to His elite.
They are not messengers,
but keepers known as "beasts."
They guard our very hope
from heaven, where we'll meet.

Promised Store

"He will keep you strong to the end so that you will be free from all blame on the day when our Lord Jesus Christ returns."
—I Corinthians 1:8

Let this day be as The Day
and each moment quietly Yours.
Let my words be as Your words,
each syllable whispering toward You.
Let my steps be as the tread
leading to Your promised store.

Delighted

"He led me to a place of safety; he rescued me because he delights in me."
—Psalm 18:19

Delighted, the glory,
the passion of One,
risen from darkness,
a new life begun.
Springing from earth
to live in the stars.
Spiritual awareness
took Him so far.
Living among us,
touching our souls,
opening our eyes,
so we could behold.
Light that now beckons,
drawing us far
to live delighted
among the stars!

A Day to Rejoice

"We grow weary in our present bodies, and we long to
put on our heavenly bodies like new clothing."
—II Corinthians 5:2

A day to remember
A day to forget
A day to stop sighing
A day to beget
A day in Your refuge
A day to bring joy
A day to flee needless
A day to rejoice

Always

"For we have heard of your faith in Christ Jesus and your love for all of God's people, which come from your confident hope of what God has reserved for you in heaven. You have had this expectation ever since you first heard the truth of the Good News."
—*Colossians 1:4-5*

In days of hope and kindness,
in years of joy contained,
we seek Your land in blindness,
concealed by robes we've stained.

The love we feel in limit,
the food we eat each day,
is now a token dimmed
by what You hold at bay.

My eyes can see a moment.
My ears can hear a sound.
Let them be opened quickly
when my feet leave the ground.

Your hand will lead forever
as I grasp it that day,
becoming Your new member,
with You always to stay.

If One Day

*"When Christ, who is your life, is revealed to the whole world,
you will share in all his glory."*
—Colossians 3:4

If one day you read this poem
and find that I am gone,
remember what I tell you,
before your life is done.
I'm on my way to see Him
and spend eternity
singing mighty praises
of His great majesty.
I'm spending my forever
sitting by His throne,
gazing at His presence,
becoming with Him as one.
I'm overwhelmed with joy,
so blessed to see His face,
weeping with thanksgiving,
basking in His grace.
I've longed to bow before Him,
to touch His garment's hem,
to feel His hands, His feet, His heart,
to praise Him once again.

You have the given choice
to sing and dance in glory.
Today, if you'll accept
the very old, old story,

you'll be with us forever.
You'll see your family.
You'll bask in loved ones' presence,
spend with them eternity.
Step out, believe in Jesus.
He's Lord and loves you so.
With Him, you'll walk on water,
as cruel winds around you blow.
You may know only heartache.
Now your soul inside you breaks.
But you can seek His great healing—
only His love wholeness makes.

When you turn your thoughts toward Him,
and you speak to Him your needs,
then you start to understand
the sowing of His seeds.
It's a life begun within you.
It's a dawning before time.
It's a newness, a beginning.
It's a powerful design.
Say, "I believe in Jesus.
He's my Lord. I love Him so.
I believe God raised Him up,
and He sits on His own throne."
With these words you have forever,
His own seed planted within.
It can grow as you allow it.
Yes, you are born again.
Seek His will, His path before you.
Listen closely for His words.
He'll direct you, if you let Him.
You are His and He is yours.

Flying

"Mounted on a mighty angelic being, he flew, soaring on the wings of the wind."
—Psalm 18:10

If you come to find me,
and you realize I am gone,
just look up to heaven,
to the clouds beyond the sun.

You'll see me riding high,
near the Master and His friends,
beaming brightly in His glory,
where my true life now begins.

I'll be smiling, laughing, singing,
to be near Him evermore.
He's my True Love, my Desire,
and beside Him I will soar.

I have always dreamed of flying,
looking down upon the world.
Then I'll have my chance to do this,
soaring way above the swirl.

Riding by a towering mountain,
flying past a cloud o'erhead,
shooting near a star that twinkles,
on His wings of wind I'll 've sped....

On a Cloud

*"Then everyone will see the Son of Man coming
on a cloud with power and great glory."*
—*Luke 21:27*

Come for us on a cloud,
when others watch and weep.
Seek us here and save us
from the world with wounds replete.

When gaping holes prevail,
and wars abound on the hill,
when floods and darkness sweep,
and men with weapons kill.

Come for us with a crown,
and eyes that shine and flash,
with a sickle in Your hand,
and glossy feet of brass.

Take us to You soon.
'Cause we watch the sky for signs
and to hear the trumpet blasts.
And every sound reminds.

How Will You Come?

"It will happen in a moment, in the blink of an eye, when the last trumpet is blown. For when the trumpet sounds, those who have died will be raised to live forever. And we who are living will also be transformed."
—I Corinthians 15:52

Will You come for us in a cloud,
when evening is quite sure,
and Your Morning Star arises,
and our flight to You endures?

Will it be like time slowed down,
when motion becomes still?
Will our hearts leap up to Yours
and every feeling thrill?

Will Your return for us be soon?
We count and count the days.
We look at every cloud
and every whitish haze.

And as the mist rolls in,
along the morning banks,
we joy in Your creation,
and to You now give thanks.

Melt

*"The mountains melt like wax before the LORD, before the Lord of all the earth.
The heavens proclaim his righteousness; every nation sees his glory."*
—Psalm 97:5-6

Will You come on a cloud
when all around us fails,
and wickedness pervades,
and fear of death prevails?

Will You shine like a star
that shoots across the skies,
and touches down on earth,
and brightens up our eyes?

Will You overwhelm us,
as we behold You then,
and gaze upon Your face,
and see where You have been?

Will Your beauty melt us,
as we discern Your glory,
and sit around Your fire,
and listen to Your story?

In Light Years

"There is an order to this resurrection: Christ was raised as the first of the harvest; then all who belong to Christ will be raised when he comes back."
—I Corinthians 15:23

In light years
we'll see Him,
Whom vanity chases,
as time or its illusion
moves us in phases,
and sadness and sorrow
it quickly erases.
Hands outstretched,
fingers reaching,
we'll be joined together,
trumpets beseeching.
In the wink of any eye,
blessedness teaching,
to the right and to the left,
clouds and sky lifting,
so fast and so far,
beautiful sifting,
bodies changing,
holiness gifting.
His face appears
as nothing we've seen,
monumental cost,
magnificent dream,
surrealistic venture,
vanishing beneath.

Forever and ever,
a new life begins.
He measures us simply,
knowing no sin,
for brand new components,
with eternal "skin."
Joyfully we celebrate.
Happily we accept.
We see our companions
never bereft,
walking on clouds
to the right and to the left.

Finally Together

"His face shone like lightning, and his clothing was as white as snow."
—Matthew 28:3

Seeking, let me seek You
in my quiet place.
Loving, let me love You,
held by Your embrace.
Pouring, let it pour down
showers of Your grace.
Raining, let it rain down
abundance in this place.
Dreaming, let me dream now
visions of Your days.
Hearing, let me hear now
trumpets in full blaze.
Seeing, let me see now
the effulgence of Your gaze.
Finally together,
with You face to face.

White Hope

"Those who trust in the LORD will find new strength. They will soar high on wings like eagles. They will run and not grow weary. They will walk and not faint."
—Isaiah 40:31

Dear One, as You listen
to my voice imploring,
bend down in Your mercy
to one who is adoring.
You've spoken with Your goodness.
You've visited inclined
to present us with a snapshot,
as we with You have dined.
In Your robes of hope-light streaming,
You rose as God's own Son
to await, with white hope gleaming,
in clouds beyond the sun.
You'll show us Your pure mercy,
when You greet Your long-lost lambs,
who'll meet You with excitement—
the ONE and GREAT I AM!

Gaze

"And they will see his face, and his name will be written on their foreheads. And there will be no night there—no need for lamps or sun—for the Lord God will shine on them. And they will reign forever and ever."
—Revelation 22:4-5

I long to see Your face,
bright shining as the sun.
I long for Your embrace,
oh mighty, glorious One.
You appeared to but a few,
as they oblivious walked.
And they did not then choose;
often their minds did balk.
But, oh, I desire so
to hold Your light-filled hand,
to behold Your brilliant glow,
to be Your biggest fan,
to walk and talk with You
along a rock-strewn path,
to climb a mountain too,
and hear Your hearty laugh,
to watch You shed a tear,
to breathe with You and sigh,
to share a secret fear,
and let hours pass us by.
Oh, to be the Apostle Paul,
who saw You when he rode,
and in his sudden fall
came into Your abode.

To be the disciples two,
walking along the road,
when You appeared so soon
and with them, questioning, strode.
To break bread and to eat
and gratefully recognize,
oh, how I long to meet
and gaze into Your eyes!

Reception

"The Spirit and the bride say, 'Come.'
Let anyone who hears this say, 'Come.' Let anyone who is thirsty come.
Let anyone who desires drink freely from the water of life."
—Revelation 22:17

Dearworthy, Beloved,
Precious One,
You died for us all,
God's significant Son.

Many despised You,
calling You names.
You forgave them all,
in the midst of Your shame.

Stand before us now worthy,
In Your rapturous robes,
glistening and sparkling,
a star to be probed.

You tower before us,
in gentleness given,
welcoming us to Your
reception in heaven.

Memories and Treasures

"He escorts me to the banquet hall; it's obvious how much he loves me."
—Song of Solomon 2:4

In her box were many treasures:
pictures, cards from long ago.
Countless memories contained in measure:
people, dreams that lived, although...
Now her body, weak and faded,
would not last as long as these.
So, she kept them hidden, dated,
'neath a sacred, pearled chemise.

On a Sunday morning early,
when she'd risen 'fore the sun,
she sought her "gifts" beneath the "pearly,"
took and read them one by one.
This one said, "I love you, Sweetie."
That one said, "I miss you so."
Another read, "Remember Italy
and your ever-loving Beau!"

As she read, her heart did flutter.
Tears came to her graying eyes.
And she barely, audibly uttered,
"Joy-filled days and binding ties."
Now only her memories served her,
as she sat upon her bed,
thankful for the twists and turnings,
and a life that lay ahead.

As wonderful as those days were seeming,
filled with travels, meals, and guests,
of a dinner she was dreaming
with the One that she loved best.
To a banquet she was headed
with a Lover, not a ghost.
To dine with Him she was quite ready,
surrounded by a heavenly host.

Fulfilled

"Let my soul be at rest again, for the LORD has been good to me. He has saved me from death, my eyes from tears, my feet from stumbling."
—Psalms 116:7-8

Son-sent mercies
Joyous gifts
Sweet encumbers
Spirit-raised lifts
Sadness ending
Sorrow flees
Senses sensing
Heartfelt peace
Blissful rapture
Grace-filled days
Mercy captured
Joy-filled spaces
Radiant blessings
Son-filled power
Trust rewarded
Fulfilled hours

Steeped

"I heard a loud shout from the throne, saying, 'Look, God's home is now among his people! He will live with them, and they will be his people. God himself will be with them. He will wipe every tear from their eyes, and there will be no more death or sorrow or crying or pain. All these things are gone forever.'"
—Revelation 21:3-4

Days of drudge and dreary
Nights of fitful rest
Moments feeling weary
Spits of light at best
Fighting thoughts of evil
Blameful, woeful times
Barely work achieving
Never feats sublime

Walking now in splendor
Enraptured in the clouds
Holding hands so tender
By great love enshrouded
Steeped in Your pure beauty
Thankfully free from pain
Appreciative of the duty
Joyful lack of shame

How You can move mountains
Rivers for us part
Changes are so sudden
Brand new, fresh new start
Thank You for this blessing
Freedom now imparted
Royal robes and dressing
Warm my once-cold heart

Unload

"Give all your worries and cares to God, for he cares about you."
—I Peter 5:7

Unload to Me your burdens.
Release to Me your cares.
Come into My kingdom,
and learn My secrets rare.
You must release your worries.
You must set free your snares,
by entering My presence
and taking time to share,
by listening very closely,
and hearing words so rare,
by speaking often to Me,
and becoming more aware
of holy spirit in you
and its true power there.
It's only through this spirit
that you will ever dare
to set free all your worries
and approach My heavenly chair.

Measured

"In the last days, the mountain of the LORD's house will be the highest of all—the most important place on earth. It will be raised above the other hills and people from all over the world will stream there to worship. People from many nations will come and say, 'Come, let us go up to the mountain of the LORD, to the house of Jacob's God. There he will teach us his ways, and we will walk in his paths.'"
—Micah 4:1-2

Mercy, humility, and kindness
are what You truly seek...
Hearts lifted up, not weighed down,
before You bowing meekly.
Pure conversations uncovered—
whisperings to You in the night.
Lowering of eyes in Your presence,
overcome by Your glorious sight.

The scales will be weighed, giving balance,
with the removal of lies and deceit.
A just measure of good, an alliance
through a hand held outstretched to heal.
Your blessing will extend to Your people,
Your favor poured out as oil.
To us You will shine out in glory.
For us You've reserved the spoil.

Micah tells of a time one day coming,
when we'll see how Your judgment falls.
And our actions and words will be measured,
as Your magnificent beauty enthralls.
Then You'll stand up so tall before us,
ruling earth as never before.
And we'll see You as You should be—
clothed in might as a rightful Warrior.

Seven Angels

"From the throne came a voice that said, 'Praise our God, all his servants, all who fear him, from the least to the greatest.'"
—Revelation 19:5

The first will bring sores
to those marked by the beast.
The second and third—
bloody rivers and seas.
The fourth one will scorch
with rays from the sun.
The fifth will cause darkness
and gnawing of tongues.
The sixth dries up water,
preparing a road.
The seventh an earthquake
and weighty hailstones.
Armageddon's the end
to everything past,
when all the god-haters
are silenced at last.

In That Day

"*As we live in God, our love grows more perfect. So we will not be afraid on the day of judgment, but we can face him with confidence because we live like Jesus here in this world.*"
—I John 4:17

You speak to me
with words of peace.
I am Your jewel—
a gem bequeathed.
And some may question
my strong stance,
and mock You now
with arrogance,
and view as idle
sound belief,
'cause rejecting right
gives them relief.
To them it's useless
to walk Your way.
They seek prosperity
in their day.
By exalting evil,
they proudly purvey
rebellion, dissension,
and a God they naysay.
But in that day,
You will declare
Your righteous treasures—
the ones You've spared.

And next to You,
I'll help select
those who chose
to not neglect.

Open this Gate

"Open the gates to all who are righteous; allow the faithful to enter."
—Isaiah 26:3

You are our strong wall.
Through You we begin
to open this gate
that welcomes us in!

You guard and You keep us
in Your perfect peace,
as our cares and worries
to You are released.

Now and forever,
we commit to You,
Rock of all ages,
lasting and true.

The way of the righteous
is level and straight.
You Who are upright,
please open this gate!

Your City

"He took me in the Spirit to a great, high mountain, and he showed me the holy city, Jerusalem, descending out of heaven from God. It shone with the glory of God and sparkled like a precious stone—like jasper as clear as crystal."
—Revelation 21:10-11

Bring to us Your City,
measured and adorned so:
with gates made of huge pearls
and insides of pure gold.
A foundation made of gems—
jasper, sapphire, agate,
emerald, onyx, ruby,
diamond, topaz, garnet,
beryl, jacinth, amethyst.
The Lord Himself shines bright
from His abode within.
The Lamb lives in His might,
with splendor never dimmed.
The nations walk in light.
And the rulers of the earth
laud Him day and night.

Palatial Place

"I can never escape from your Spirit! I can never get away from your presence! If I go up to heaven, you are there; if I go down to the grave, you are there. If I ride the wings of the morning, if I dwell by the farthest oceans, even there your hand will guide me, and your strength will support me."
—Psalm 139:7-12

Special is Your favor.
Gem-filled is Your hand.
Righteous is our pleasure
in Your lovely land.
Succored by Your presence.
Enraptured by Your grace.
Surrounded by Your glory
in Your palatial place.

Magnificent One

"His body looked like a precious gem. His face flashed like lightning, and his eyes flamed like torches. His arms and feet shone like polished bronze, and his voice roared like a vast multitude of people."
—Daniel 10:6

I have heard of Your beauty—
how You outshine the sun.
I have read of Your glory,
oh, Magnificent One!

How You're clad with fine topaz
and sardius bright red,
how Your clothes are bedecked
from Your feet to Your head.

How Your breast wrapped with gold,
and Your feet of bright bronze,
cannot be imagined,
oh, Beautiful One!

Most glorious of all,
I have read of Your hair—
bright white like fine snow,
it can't be compared.

How Your robe cascades down
and Your eyes flash like fire,
how Your voice is like waves,
oh, how You I desire!

Most amazingly still,
I have heard of Your face—
how it glows like the sun
in full force at midday.

You sound so fantastic,
and I long so to be
in Your presence, my Beauty,
for eternity!

Abounding

*"We are citizens of heaven, where the Lord Jesus Christ lives.
And we are eagerly waiting for him to return as our Savior."*
—Philippians 3:20

Strength is in numbers,
many might say.
Strength is in money,
fortune, and fame.
No, said the wise man,
Strength is in love.
Strength is in blessings
bestowed from above.
Perhaps when we're honest,
perhaps when we're real,
we may see a small glimpse
of what he does mean.
Look a bit closer,
behind what you see,
beneath the wide surface,
beyond what you hear.
You'll see a forever.
You'll hear it foretold.
It's not a new story,
but one very old.
It started so long
before you were born.
It will last 'til a time
unknown, I am told.
See a home, see a future

where you can dwell.
In a land full of beauty
far, far beyond hell.
There we will walk together
side by side, arm in arm,
laughing and singing,
beyond peril's harm.
You and me merrily
with grace surrounding.
Never, ever a need.
In His love abounding.

Oh

"Then Jesus climbed a hill and sat down with his disciples around him."
—*John 6:3*

Oh, the stories You will tell,
sitting with us for a spell,
drinking wine and eating bread,
opening books we've never read.

Oh, the light You will reveal,
sharing with us Your full meal,
talking until who knows when,
explaining miracles once again.

Oh, the fellowship You will share,
revealing thoughts and words so rare,
relating worlds so far beyond,
leaving us dumbfounded with sighs and nods.

My Deepest Desire

"Then I heard every creature in heaven and on earth and under the earth and in the sea. They sang: 'Blessing and honor and glory and power belong to the one sitting on the throne and to the Lamb forever and ever.'"
—Revelation 5:13

I want to be in the front row
with family by my side,
singing praises, holding hands,
gazing up into Your eyes.

I want to celebrate with You,
and others whom I love,
and listen to all Your stories—
Your revelation treasure trove.

Oh, bring their hearts once more to You,
so with them I can sigh,
and hug, and share our memories,
as we all laugh and cry.

How Wonderful

"Such knowledge is too wonderful for me, too great for me to understand!"
—Psalm 139:6

How wonderful You are in all Your ways!
How magical t'will be to hear You say,
"I love your heart, your life, your earth-spent days!
And how you tried with all your might to praise."

Someday we'll be together endlessly.
And I'll be next to You eternally.
I'll gaze beyond the rainbow ardently.
And then I'll understand the meaning finally.

Read other books by Lele Beutel, sign up for her newsletter, and follow on social media by scanning the QR code or going to the URL below:

linktr.ee/authorlelebeutel

About the Author

Lele Beutel and her husband, Mike, enjoy traveling to new places. They have found that with each excursion come opportunities to make a difference in people's lives and have their own lives changed by others. Walking on the Camino de Santiago was one such adventure for Lele. She considers herself to be "secret agent" for God because of how He often leads her into unexpected situations where she's able to connect with others. Before retirement, she spent 25 years as a financial advisor and was able to encourage many people mentally, spiritually, and financially through her faith-based advice. Now, she and her husband spend time with their two dogs, Andey and Barney, with grandkids, and as volunteers at their church. They also share experiences with their life group members and the neighbors they meet while walking the dogs.

Other books she has written include: *What God Wants You to Know*, a 365-day devotional that reveals God's heart relating to passages from Genesis through Revelation; *From a Secret Place*, a daily devotional with questions and answers to and from God that came from 20 years of journaling; *The Reignbreaker*, a young adult fantasy; *Flora's Story*, about a young German refugee who miraculously escapes and survives the Nazi and Russian regimes of WWII Germany; and three books of poetry: *Lele's Lovesongs: Words of hope for the ones we love*; *Lele's Sighs: Reflections and Recollections*; and *The Camino Connection: Connecting with Life and Commemorating a Death While Walking on the Camino de Santiago*.

To reach her, you can find her on Facebook. Or email her at: apedersen6@comcast.net

She would love to hear from you!